First World War

and Army of Occupation

War Diary

France, Belgium and Germany

27 DIVISION
Divisional Troops
17 Field Company Royal Engineers
1 April 1915 - 31 December 1915

WO95/2258/1

The Naval & Military Press Ltd
www.nmarchive.com
Published in association with The National Archives

Published by

The Naval & Military Press Ltd

Unit 10 Ridgewood Industrial Park,

Uckfield, East Sussex,

TN22 5QE England

Tel: +44 (0) 1825 749494

www.naval-military-press.com

www.nmarchive.com

This diary has been reprinted in facsimile from the original. Any imperfections are inevitably reproduced and the quality may fall short of modern type and cartographic standards.

Contents

Document type	Place/Title	Date From	Date To
Heading	WO95/2258-1		
Heading	17th Field Coy R.E. Apr-Dec 1915		
Heading	17th Field Coy RE Vol IX 1-30.4.15		
Heading	War Diary of 17th Field Company RE April 1st to April 30th 1915		
War Diary		01/04/1915	01/04/1915
War Diary	Ypres	02/04/1915	09/04/1915
War Diary	Potijze	10/04/1915	30/04/1915
Heading	17th Coy R.E. Vol X 1-31.5.15		
Heading	War Diary of 17th Field Company RE From May 1st 1915 to May 31st 1915		
War Diary	Potijze	01/05/1915	04/05/1915
War Diary	Vlamertinghe	05/05/1915	31/05/1915
Heading	27th Division 17th Field Coy RE Vol XI 1-30.6.15		
Heading	17th Field Company RE. From June 1st 1915 to June 30th 1915		
War Diary		01/06/1915	01/06/1915
War Diary	Amentieres	02/06/1915	30/06/1915
Heading	27th Division 17th Field Coy RE Vol XII		
Heading	War Diary Of 17 Field Coy RE For Period July 1st to 31st 1915		
War Diary		01/07/1915	31/07/1915
Heading	17th Field Coy RE Vol XIII		
Heading	War Diary of 17th Field Company RE For period Aug 1st to 31st 1915		
War Diary	Armentiers	01/08/1915	29/08/1915
War Diary	Rue Marle Armentieres	30/08/1915	31/08/1915
Heading	17th Field Coy RE Vol XIV Sept 15		
Heading	War Diary of 17 Field Coy. RE. For Period 1st Sept to 30th Sept 1915		
War Diary	Billets at Rue Marle Armentieres	01/09/1915	14/09/1915
War Diary	Strazeele	15/09/1915	30/09/1915
Heading	17th Field Coy RE Vol XV Oct 15		
Heading	War Diary of 17th Field Coy RE for Period Oct 1st 1915 to Oct 31st 1915		
War Diary	Cappy	01/10/1915	31/10/1915
Heading	17th Fc. Co. RE. Nov Vol XVI		
Heading	War Diary Of 17th Field Coy RE. For Period Nov 1st to 30th 1915		
War Diary	Fluy	01/11/1915	30/11/1915
Heading	17th Fc. Co. RE. Dec Vol. XVII		
War Diary	Fluy	01/12/1915	08/12/1915
War Diary	Marseilles	09/12/1915	31/12/1915

27TH DIVISION
DIVL ENGINEERS

17TH FIELD COY R.E.

APR - DEC 1915

FROM 5 DIV

27th Divn

121/5161

17th Field Coy: RE

Vol IX 1–30. 4. 15

Army Form C. 2118.

Instructions regarding War Diaries and Intelligence Summaries are contained in F. S. Regs., Part II. and the Staff Manual respectively. Title pages will be prepared in manuscript.

WAR DIARY
or
INTELLIGENCE SUMMARY
(Erase heading not required.)

Hour, Date, Place	Summary of Events and Information	Remarks and references to Appendices
	Confidential War Diary of 17th Field Company R.E. from April 1st to April 30th 1915. C. W. Singer [?] Major R.E. Comdg 17th Fld. Coy. R.E. [signature] Lt Col C.R.E. 27th Div	

1247 W 3299 200,000 (E) 8/14 J.B.C. & A. Forms/C. 2118/11.

Instructions regarding War Diaries and Intelligence Summaries are contained in F. S. Regs., Part II. and the Staff Manual respectively. Title pages will be prepared in manuscript.

WAR DIARY
or
INTELLIGENCE SUMMARY.
(Erase heading not required.)

Army Form C. 2118.

Hour, Date, Place	Summary of Events and Information	Remarks and References to Appendices
April 1st 1915	Billet at station at YPRES.	
	Night Nos 1 & 3 sects. (Lts. Hall & Pottinger) to work on 2nd line south of Ypres at 6 pm, returning at 5 am. Wire entanglement completed & revetments for parados continued.	
April 2nd 1915. Ypres	Night (second line) No 2 sect. (Lt. Godsell) & 3 NCOs of No 1 sect. (Lt. Fowle) continued revetment of parados & two reliefs of 500 inf. filled in parados.	
	Maj Singer & Capt Spackman went round 82nd Brigade trenches S. of Menin Road with Gen Longley	
	Lt. Hall took charge of mines in the above trenches for 24 hours	
April 3rd 1915 Ypres	Day Nos. 1, 3 & 4 sects. went for route march in morning.	
	Night. No 3 sect. (Lt. Pottinger) on second line completed revetments of parados, which was filled in by infantry	

(9 29 6) W 3332—1107 100,000 10/13 H W V Forms/C. 2118/10.

Army Form C. 2118.

Instructions regarding War Diaries and Intelligence Summaries are contained in F. S. Regs., Part II. and the Staff Manual respectively. Title pages will be prepared in manuscript.

WAR DIARY
or
INTELLIGENCE SUMMARY.
(Erase heading not required.)

Hour, Date, Place	Summary of Events and Information	Remarks and References to Appendices
April 4th 1915 Ypres	Company went for route march in morning to ELVERDINGHE.	
April 5th 1915 Ypres	Route march in morning. Maj. Singer went round 80th Brig. trenches with Gen. Smith in afternoon.	
April 6th 1915 Ypres	Route march in morning. Lt. Fowle reported to O.C. 2nd Wessex R.E. for temporary duty with them as they were short of officers.	
April 7th 1915 Ypres	No. 3 sect. (Lt. Pottinger) took over huts behind trenches from French. Maj. Singer & Lt Godsell went round support trenches in afternoon.	
April 8th 1915 Ypres	No 3 sect. (Lt Pottinger) in trenches improving communications, manning listening galleries – improving loopholes. Remainder of company pontooning.	
April 9th 1915 Ypres.	No. 2 sect (Lt. Godsell) joined No 3 sect in trenches – Manning listening Galleries, wiring posts, preparing loopholes, improving communications, siting & marking out new support trenches. Remainder of Coy. route march & pontooning. Billet was shelled from 2 to 4 pm. one driver being killed in stable & two wounded. Dr. Trotter was killed on Menin road while bringing Lt Fowle's horse home.	Casualties. 19732 Sapr. Taylor G. killed in trenches. 23695 Dr. Devlin wounded) by Shell 14531 " O'Grady killed } in billets. 20440 Dr. Trotter T. killed by shell in Menin Road while returning with Lt. Fowle's horse from HOOGE

Instructions regarding War Diaries and Intelligence Summaries are contained in F. S. Regs., Part II. and the Staff Manual respectively. Title pages will be prepared in manuscript.

WAR DIARY
or
INTELLIGENCE SUMMARY.
(*Erase heading not required.*)

Army Form C. 2118.

Hour, Date, Place	Summary of Events and Information	Remarks and References to Appendices
April 10th 1915. POTIJZE	Moved into huts at POTIJZE, 3/4 miles East of Ypres in afternoon. 2 sections in trenches as on 9th continued same work. Remainder of company pontooning in morning, before changing billet.	
April 11th 1915. POTIJZE.	No1 sect (Lt. Hall) relieved No3 sect. (Lt. Pottinger) in trenches in morning – making loopholes, communication trench & machine gun emplacement at night; Day: Building magazine, improving roads Officers billet moved across road out of 28th Div. area.	
April 12th 1915 POTIJZE.	Two sections in trenches as on 11th work – Night. New commun. trench dug from left of C Trench to wood. Extreme left trench drained. M.G. emplacement re-constructed & Infantry assisted with wiring & improving parapet. Day Improving road, cutting pickets & assisting infantry in making "knife rests". The 2 sects from POTIJZE constructed huts for Reserve Companies in ~~Nonne~~ Bosscher wood.	

Army Form C. 2118.

Instructions regarding War Diaries and Intelligence Summaries are contained in F. S. Regs., Part II. and the Staff Manual respectively. Title pages will be prepared in manuscript.

WAR DIARY
or
INTELLIGENCE SUMMARY.
(Erase heading not required.)

Hour, Date, Place	Summary of Events and Information	Remarks and References to Appendices
April 13th 1915 POTIJZE.	No 4 sect (Lt. Fowle) relieved No 2 sect (Lt Gotsell) in trenches:— Lt. Fowle returned to work with company in afternoon, after temporary duty with 2nd Wessex Fld. Coy & joined his section in trenches.	Casualties. 11475 Spr. Graham J. wounded in trenches.
	Night New communication trench ~~was~~ revetted, MG emplacement constructed, & loopholes made.	
	Day Repairing road, making bridges to new dumping ground & revetting 2nd Subsidiary line	
April 14th 1915	Two sects. in trenches as on 13th	Casualty. 8827 Spr. Heathcote wounded in trenches.
	Night Revetting parapet, making loopholes & M.G. emplacement — supervising infantry on Commn trench from front line & constructing parados on 2nd subsidiary line.	
	Day Improving road & revetting 2nd Sub. Line	

Instructions regarding War Diaries and Intelligence Summaries are contained in F. S. Regs., Part II. and the Staff Manual respectively. Title pages will be prepared in manuscript.

WAR DIARY
or
INTELLIGENCE SUMMARY.
(*Erase heading not required.*)

Army Form C. 2118.

Hour, Date, Place	Summary of Events and Information	Remarks and References to Appendices
April 15th 1915 POTIJZE.	No. 3 Sect (Lt. Pottinger) relieved No. 1 sect. (Lt. Hall) in trenches.	
	Day widening trench in 2nd line, Repairing path, revetting 2nd line trenches.	
	Night Revetting support trench breastwork & supervising infantry on commun. trenches & making banquet in fire trenches.	
	Orders to stand by & harness up horses at 6pm. owing to possibility of attack.	
April 16th 1915.	Two sects. in trenches as on 15th.	
	Night. All inf. working parties cancelled owing to fear of attack. Sects. revetted parapet of support trench on left.	
	Day Repairing road & path, revetting 2nd line trenches	
	Nos. 1 & 2 sects. from billets revetted 2nd line trenches.	
	Capt. Spackman reconnoitred French subsidiary line	
April 17th 1915.	Two sects. in support trenches as on 15th.	
	Night Revetting commun. trenches 74-75a, 75a-75b. Inf on 2nd line supervised.	
	Day Repairing road, revetting 2nd line.	
	Sects. in billets made position for trench mortar, & prepared stand for rifle battery. 1 NCO & 10 sappers loading up at R.E. Store.	

(9 29 6) W 3332—1107 100,000 10/13 H W V Forms/C. 2118/10.

Instructions regarding War Diaries and Intelligence Summaries are contained in F. S. Regs., Part II, and the Staff Manual respectively. Title pages will be prepared in manuscript.

WAR DIARY
or
INTELLIGENCE SUMMARY.
(*Erase heading not required.*)

Army Form C. 2118.

Hour, Date, Place	Summary of Events and Information	Remarks and References to Appendices
April 18th 1915. POTIJZE	Two sects. in support trenches as on 15th Night. Revetting communication trench. Day. Repairs to road. Remainder of company bathing in Ypres	
April 19th 1915.	No1 sect. (Lt. Hall) relieves No3 sect. (Lt. Pottinger) in trenches. Night Repairing road + making loopholes with infantry working parties. Day Repairing roads + revetting 2nd Line. Remainder of Coy. revetting 2nd line + repairing Bath, Ypres.	Casualties. 22396 Spr. Rhodes H. Killed in trenches. 7968 Spr. McDonald died of shock on Menin Road.
April 20th 1915.	Two sects. in trenches as on 19th Night Supervising inf. on commun. trenches, breastworks + 2nd line, + continued work on road. Day Constructing magazine + revetting 2nd line. Remainder of Coy. (No 3 + 4 sects.) pontooning on moat at Ypres.	
April 21st 1915.	No4 sect. (Lt. Fowle) relieves No2 sect. (Lt. Godsell) in trenches. Night. Supervising infantry on support breastworks + commun. trenches. Day Completed magazine, revetting 2nd line; Remainder of Coy. - No3 sect. (Lt. Pottinger) started work on Brigadiers' dugouts	21653 Spr. James H. wounded

Instructions regarding War Diaries and Intelligence Summaries are contained in F. S. Regs., Part II. and the Staff Manual respectively. Title pages will be prepared in manuscript.

WAR DIARY
or
INTELLIGENCE SUMMARY
(Erase heading not required.)

Army Form C. 2118.

Hour, Date, Place	Summary of Events and Information	Remarks and references to Appendices
April 22nd 1915. POTIJZE.	2 sects in trenches as on 21st. Night Assisting Infantry on Communication & Support Breastworks & trenches – revetting breastworks. Day Revetting 2nd Line, repairing road. Remainder from billets ~~completing~~ making Brigadiers dug-out & revetting 2nd line	
April 23rd 1915.	No 3 sect. (Lt. Pottinger) relieved No 1 sect. (Lt. Hall) in trenches Night Revetting breastwork, supervising infantry filling in Day Erecting rifle battery at NONNE BOSCHEN wood. Revetting & marking out 2nd Line – erecting hut as dressing station. Remainder of Coy constructing Brigadiers dug-out, & dug-outs for company at ~~[illegible]~~ POTIJZE	

1247 W 3299 200,000 (E) 8/14 J.B.C. & A. Forms/C. 2118/11.

Instructions regarding War Diaries and Intelligence Summaries are contained in F. S. Regs., Part II. and the Staff Manual respectively. Title pages will be prepared in manuscript.

Army Form C. 2118.

WAR DIARY
or
INTELLIGENCE SUMMARY

(Erase heading not required.)

Hour, Date, Place	Summary of Events and Information	Remarks and references to Appendices
April 24th 1915 POTIJZE	Two sects in trenches as on 23rd Night working on Switch line along NONNE BOSCHEN WOOD Nos 1 & 2 sects (Lt. Hall & Godsell) went out at 7.45 pm with 2 sects each of 1st Wessex & 2nd Wessex Fld Coys & were joined by the 2 sects from the trenches for this work. also manning listening galleries in Brigade trenches. Day Laying mines in trenches, & repairing road.	Casualty. 13322 Spr. G. Simpson wounded.
April 25th 1915.	Two sects in trenches as on 23rd Night Arranging land mines & revetting support trenches. Remainder of coy making dug-outs at billets, removing explosives from R.E. Store at Ypres, & digging cover trenches at Chateau at POTIJZE for a Brigade coming up as reinforcement.	24937 Spr. T. Wigson wounded 23944 Spr. Cadman C killed 19946 Spr. Chilwell wounded 24794 Spr. Ward killed.
April 26th 1915.	Two sects in trenches as on 23rd Day Assisting infantry in wiring Switch Line along NONNE BOSCHEN WOOD Night Continuing days' work Remainder of Coy. making new dug outs at billets.	20261 Dr. Winch killed 17762 a/Corpl Hards wounded 18713 Spr Thompson killed (by shell in billets.)

Instructions regarding War Diaries and Intelligence Summaries are contained in F. S. Regs., Part II. and the Staff Manual respectively. Title pages will be prepared in manuscript.

WAR DIARY
or
INTELLIGENCE SUMMARY
(Erase heading not required.)

Army Form C. 2118.

Hour, Date, Place	Summary of Events and Information	Remarks and references to Appendices
April 27th 1915. POTIJZE	Lt Hall + 3 NCOs of No1 sect joined the two sects. in trenches in evening, & remained there Night Supervising & assisting infantry on "Switch" line. Day Repairs to road. Remainder of Coy on dug outs at Billets.	Casualties 18825 Dr. Watkins wounded 2733 Spr Skillet T. " (by shell in billets). 28th 21088 Dr. Isson wounded
April 28th 1915 POTIJZE.	Remainder of No1 sect relieved No3 sect in trenches Day Repairs to road; Night Assisting infantry on Switch Line, & wiring, & continuing work on 2nd Subsidiary line. Remainder of Coy improving & making new dug-outs at billets.	12581 Dr. Hussey P. " 13573 a/Sergt Rogers C. wounded 10346 Spr Shaw " 28321 Spr Porter T. " 1626 Spr Wilson " 12302 Spr Bondy " (by shell in billet).
April 29th 1915. POTIJZE.	Two sects. in trenches as on 28th. Day ~~work~~ Cutting pickets for night work. Night work continued on Switch & subsidiary lines with infantry; - wiring & revetting. Remainder of Coy. improving dug outs at billets.	

1247 W 3299 200,000 (E) 8/14 J.B.C. & A. Forms/C. 2118/11.

Instructions regarding War Diaries and Intelligence Summaries are contained in F. S. Regs., Part II. and the Staff Manual respectively. Title pages will be prepared in manuscript.

WAR DIARY
or
INTELLIGENCE SUMMARY
(Erase heading not required.)

Army Form C. 2118.

Hour, Date, Place	Summary of Events and Information	Remarks and references to Appendices
April 30th 1915. POTIJZE.	Two sects. in trenches as on 28th Day Preparing for night work Night Nos 3 & 4 sects. (Lts. Pottinger & Fowle) joined by the 2 sects (Nos 1 & 2) from the trenches supervised the infantry party (1500) on the new 'Switch' Line from HOOGE CHATEAU to the railway, & started the wiring during the afternoon – this was completed at night by the 4th Div. Engineers (Maj. Hoysted RE.) under the supervision of Maj. Singer. Remainder of Coy. – supplied loading party for lorry carrying pickets & wire to HOOGE for night work. Note from the 22nd April until the end of the month, the German attack on the French north of Ypres having started on the evening of the 22nd, the huts & dug-outs occupied by the company at POTIJZE were continually under heavy shell fire	Casualty. 13986 Spr. Crees B.F. Killed (by shell in billets).

1247 W 3299 200,000 (E) 8/14 J.B.C. & A. Forms/C. 2118/11.

24th Division

121/5554

17th Coy: R.E

Vol X 1 — 31.5.15

187.
DTW

Army Form C. 2118.

Instructions regarding War Diaries and Intelligence Summaries are contained in F. S. Regs., Part II. and the Staff Manual respectively. Title pages will be prepared in manuscript.

WAR DIARY
or
INTELLIGENCE SUMMARY.

(*Erase heading not required.*)

Hour, Date, Place	Summary of Events and Information	Remarks and references to Appendices
	Confidential War diary of 17th Field Company R.E. from May 1st 1915 to May 31st 1915. C. W. Singer [signature] Major R.E. Commanding 17th Field Company R.E.	

Instructions regarding War Diaries and Intelligence Summaries are contained in F. S. Regs., Part II. and the Staff Manual respectively. Title pages will be prepared in manuscript.

WAR DIARY
or
INTELLIGENCE SUMMARY
(Erase heading not required.)

Army Form C. 2118.

Hour, Date, Place	Summary of Events and Information	Remarks and references to Appendices
May 1st 1915 POTIJZE	4 Sects in support trenches. ~~[illegible]~~ (Lts Pottinger, Fowle Godsell & Hall.) Maj. Sniger remained at 80th Brig. Hqrs.	Casualties. ~~wounded.~~ 17560 L. Cpl. Swaddling A. 18844 Sap. Hawthorne J. wounded while working in trenches.
	Day. Preparation for, & laying out trenches for night work.	
	Night. Supervising & assisting infantry on Switch line from Roulers Railway, North of Bellewarde Lake, to Menin Road East of HOOGE	
May 2nd 1915.	No 1, 2 & 3 sects in support trenches - No 4 sect. (Lieut. Fowle) returned to POTIJZE at 3.30 am.	
	Night. Work continued on switch line as on 1st. Capt. Spackman & Lt. Fowle supervised infantry party clearing roadway & bridge at Menin Gate.	
May 3rd 1915.	Nos 1, 2 & 3 sects in Support trenches	
	Day. Work continued on new switch line & making dugouts.	
	Night. Supervising infantry on 'switch', & preparing mines in Polygon Wood	

1247 W 3299 200,000 (E) 8/14 J.B.C. & A. Forms/C. 2118/11.

Instructions regarding War Diaries and Intelligence Summaries are contained in F. S. Regs., Part II. and the Staff Manual respectively. Title pages will be prepared in manuscript.

WAR DIARY
or
INTELLIGENCE SUMMARY

(Erase heading not required.)

Army Form C. 2118.

Hour, Date, Place	Summary of Events and Information	Remarks and references to Appendices
May 4th 1915.	No 2 sect joined Hd Qrs at POTIJZE during night 3/4. Nos 2 & 4 sects. (Lt Godsell & Fowle) went to work at 4 am. & joined by Nos 1 & 3 sects. continued work on New Switch, revetting & wiring.	Casualties: Lieut. C.E.R. Pottinger RE. Severely wounded while leaving front trenches, by Shrapnell in Bellewarde wood. 13432 2nd Cpl. (act. Sergt.) Carter J. Killed.
	Hd. Qrs & mounted section (Capt. Shackman) moved to VLAMARTINGE, leaving POTIJZE in two parties at 6 am & 6.30 am., & were joined there by Nos 2 & 4 sects (Lt Godsell & Fowle) on their return from work with the 80th Brig.	19308 Sap. Allan W. Killed. 24083 Sap. Bellemie A. Killed by Shell behind trenches. 26171 Sap. Sergeant C. wounded. 25587 Sap. Spindler B. "
May 5th 1915. Vlamartinghe	Two sections in support trenches:– No 4 sect. (Lt Fowle) relieved No 1 sect. (Lt. Hall) in support trenches during night.	13031 Sap. Walters H. " 25757 Sap. Hale D. " 2290 Sap. Goldsmith E. " by Shell when working near HOOGE.
	Day Two sects. in support continued work on new Switch line. Two sects at Vlamartinghe started work on dugouts for company there. ~~Lieut C.E.R. Pottinger was severely wounded while returning from work [illegible] trenches near Bellewarde wood.~~	May 6th 1915. 16076 2/Cpl. Fleming P. Slightly wounded while checking [illegible] on Menin Road.

1247 W 3299 200,000 (E) 8/14 J.B.C. & A. Forms/C. 2118/11.

Instructions regarding War Diaries and Intelligence Summaries are contained in F. S. Regs., Part II. and the Staff Manual respectively. Title pages will be prepared in manuscript.

WAR DIARY
or
INTELLIGENCE SUMMARY
(Erase heading not required.)

Army Form C. 2118.

Hour, Date, Place	Summary of Events and Information	Remarks and references to Appendices
May 6th 1915. Vlamertinghe	Day. Two sects with Hdqrs. making dug outs for company at Vlamertinghe.	
	Two sects in support moved to cellars opposite Ecole de Bienfaisance on Menin Road.	
May 7th 1915.	Night. No 4 sect (Lt Fowle) started work on Dug-outs near railway crossing South of Port de Lille for Signallers, No 1 sect (Lt Hall) from Vlamertinghe completing them at 4 am.	
May 8th 1915.	Day. Work continued on dug outs at Vlamertinghe.	
	Night. Two sects with 80th Brig. working on GHQ. line and support trenches in front line. No 2 sect. (Lt Godsell) relieved No 3 sect. (Capt. Macdonald) with 80th Brig. at 4 am.	
	Day. Remainder of Coy continued work on dugouts at Vlamertinghe.	

1247 W 3299 200,000 (E) 8/14 J.B.C. & A. Forms/C. 2118/11.

Instructions regarding War Diaries and Intelligence Summaries are contained in F. S. Regs., Part II. and the Staff Manual respectively. Title pages will be prepared in manuscript.

WAR DIARY
or
INTELLIGENCE SUMMARY
(Erase heading not required.)

Army Form C. 2118.

Hour, Date, Place	Summary of Events and Information	Remarks and references to Appendices
May 9th 1915. Vlamartinghe.	Night Nos 1 & 3 secs. (Lt Hall) joined Maj. Singer with 80th Brig. ~~bus~~ at 11pm. but owing to a change in orders, were not required for work.	Casualties. Lieut G. F. Hall R.E. (S.R.) slightly wounded by Shrapnell in billet on Menin road
	No 2 & 4 secs (Lts. Godsell & Fowle) wiring & revetting new line North of Bellewaarde Lake this line was abandoned early in the morning.	1938 Sap. Matthews E. Killed 16466 " Barker W. " while wiring in front of trenches
	Day On return from night work, Capt Sparkman reconnoitred bridge in square 13a near Ypres railway Stn. & this was prepared for demolition during afternoon by Lieut Hall.	~~[illegible]~~ 13152 L Cpl. Vickery J. wounded 25975 Sap. Geelan P. " 22508 " Patrick J. " 18751 " Jones. J "
May 10th 1915.	2Lt. C. A. Coombs joined & took over No 3 section. No 1 sect. (Lt. Hall) ~~[illegible]~~ relieved No 4 sect. with 80th Brig. Lt. Hall was slightly wounded by shrapnell in house on Menin road soon after getting there & returned in evening to Vlamartinghe. No 3 sect. continued work on dug-outs for 80 & 81st Brigs. on Dickebusch bed (square 18c) which had been started by Capt Noble & 1st Wessex Fld. coy.	16463. Sap Gardner T.

Instructions regarding War Diaries and Intelligence Summaries are contained in F. S. Regs., Part II. and the Staff Manual respectively. Title pages will be prepared in manuscript.

WAR DIARY
or
INTELLIGENCE SUMMARY
(Erase heading not required.)

Army Form C. 2118.

Hour, Date, Place	Summary of Events and Information	Remarks and references to Appendices
May 11th 1915. Vlamertinghe	Night. Nos 1 & 2 sects. (~~Lt [illegible]~~ Lt. Godsell) ~~[illegible]~~ worked on Bellewarde Farm, placing it in a state of defence & wired it, & dug support trench behind wood with infantry working party. Nos 3 & 4 sects. joined above at 7pm with the 80th Brig. and dug trenches parallel to Menin road, filling gap on left of 81st Brig. Day. No work, as whole company had been out for the previous night.	Casualty 28373 Sap. McKay. J. wounded while wiring near Bellewarde Lake. Lieut. Pottinger died at Base, from wounds received on the 4th.
May 12th 1915. Vlamertinghe	Night. Nos 3 & 4 sects. (Lt. Coombs & Fowle) joined the 2 sects. with the 80th Brigade at 7pm. and placed HOOGE Chateau in a state of defence, dug support trench west of BELLEGARDE Wood & made a barricade across railway. No 4 sect (Lt. Fowle) relieved No 2 section. Day Making two additional huts for sections due to return from the 80th Brig.	Casualties 18219 Sap. Cree A. Killed by shrapnel on Menin Rd while cyclist orderly.

Instructions regarding War Diaries and Intelligence Summaries are contained in F. S. Regs., Part II. and the Staff Manual respectively. Title pages will be prepared in manuscript.

WAR DIARY
or
INTELLIGENCE SUMMARY
(Erase heading not required.)

Army Form C. 2118.

Hour, Date, Place	Summary of Events and Information	Remarks and references to Appendices
May 13th - 1915 Vlamartinghe.	Two sections at Vlamartinghe were placed under orders of C.E. 5th Corps, for work on Zillebeke line. No 1 sect. (Lt. Hall) came in from 80th Brig. at 10 pm, leaving one section (No 4, Lt Fowle) with Major Singer there. Night No 3 & 4 sects. (Lts Coombs & Fowle) joined sects with 80th Brig; - put HOOGE CHATEAU in state of defence, wired it, & made barricade across railway	
May 14th - 1915.	Night No 2 & 3 sects. (Capt Spackman, Lts Godsell & Coombs) working on Zillebeke Switch under C.E. - dug 3 support trenches, wiring continued, hedgefields partially cleared and 2 houses on Zillebeke road demolished with guncotton. No 1 & 4 sects. (Lt. Godsell) with 80th Brig continued & finished placing Hooge Chateau in state of defence, & wired it, a section of the 2nd Wessex finishing work begun by 17 Coy on the support trench behind Bellegarde wood.	

Instructions regarding War Diaries and Intelligence Summaries are contained in F. S. Regs., Part II. and the Staff Manual respectively. Title pages will be prepared in manuscript.

WAR DIARY
or
INTELLIGENCE SUMMARY
(Erase heading not required.)

Army Form C. 2118.

Hour, Date, Place	Summary of Events and Information	Remarks and references to Appendices
May 15th 1915. Vlamertinghe	No 3 sect. (Lt. Coombs.) relieved No 4 sect. (Lt Fowle) with the 80th Brig.	
	Day No 4 section completed huts in billets begun the previous day in afternoon.	
	Night No 3 & 4 sects (Lt. Coombs & Fowle) with 200 of 4th Bn K. Yorks dug & wired trench from Bellewaarde Fm. to Railway.	
May 16th 1915. Vlamertinghe	Day Lt Godsell supervised infantry party working on canal line.	
	Night No 2 sect. (Lt Godsell) went to 80 Brig. Hdqrs at 5.30 pm worked there during night, and relieved No 3 sect. (Lt Coombs) which returned to Vlamertinghe at 4 am. Trench wire put in front of trench dug on previous night from Bellewaarde Fm. to Railway.	

Instructions regarding War Diaries and Intelligence Summaries are contained in F. S. Regs., Part II. and the Staff Manual respectively. Title pages will be prepared in manuscript.

WAR DIARY
or
INTELLIGENCE SUMMARY
(Erase heading not required.)

Army Form C. 2118.

Hour, Date, Place	Summary of Events and Information	Remarks and references to Appendices
May 17th 1915 Vlamertinghe	Night. No 1 & No 4 sects (Lt Hall & Fowle) on Zillebeke line with 600 infantry. Widened front trenches, dug communication to lake, wired round brickfields, & made 4 Machine Gun emplacements, & demolished house on Zillebeke road Major Singer & No 2 section (Lt. Godsell) returned from 80th Brig. during evening, the 80 Brig. being relieved by cavalry.	Casualties. 18021 Sap. Patterson W. wounded in Hooge wood. 7870 Sap. Stevens. J. do
May 18th 1915	Night. No 3 sect (Lt Coombs) on Zillebeke line at 6.30 pm., finished wiring front trenches. 400 infantry, who should have been met at Bienfaisance school at 8.15 pm., did not eventuate	

1247 W 3299 200,000 (E) 8/14 J.B.C. & A. Forms/C. 2118/11.

Instructions regarding War Diaries and Intelligence Summaries are contained in F. S. Regs., Part II. and the Staff Manual respectively. Title pages will be prepared in manuscript.

WAR DIARY
or
INTELLIGENCE SUMMARY
(Erase heading not required.)

Army Form C. 2118.

Hour, Date, Place	Summary of Events and Information	Remarks and references to Appendices
May 19th 1915 Vlamertinghe	Night Nos 1 + 2 sects (Lt Hall + Godsell) on Zillebeke line with 400 infantry. Sandbagging parapet of fire trenches, digging cover trenches 5x behind fire trenches. The company was placed under orders of CRE Cav. Corps (Maj Sandys)	
May 20th 1915	Night Nos 3 + 4 sects (Lt Coombs + Fowle) on Zillebeke line, with 400 inf., digging cover trenches + sandbagging parapet	Casualty
May 21st 1915	Night Nos 1 + 2 sects (Lt Hall + Godsell) on Zillebeke line, Sandbagging parapet, no infantry being available	13255 Sap. Heavyside ? wounded on Zillebeke line
May 22nd 1915	Night Nos 3 + 4 sects (Lt Coombs + Fowle) continued work on Zillebeke line as on 21st	21720 Sap. Kennedy W. wounded on Zillebeke line

1247 W 3299 200,000 (E) 8/14 J.B.C. & A. Forms/C. 2118/11.

Army Form C. 2118.

Instructions regarding War Diaries and Intelligence Summaries are contained in F. S. Regs., Part II. and the Staff Manual respectively. Title pages will be prepared in manuscript.

WAR DIARY
or
INTELLIGENCE SUMMARY
(Erase heading not required.)

Hour, Date, Place	Summary of Events and Information	Remarks and references to Appendices
May 23rd 1915 Vlamartinghe	Night No 1 & 2 secs. (Lt. Hall & Godsell) on Zillebeke line with 600 cavalry. Completed sandbagging parapet of cover trenches, dug 3 new support trenches and 2 commun. trenches, & widened & deepened cover trenches to 5 ft. deep.	
May 24th 1915 Vlamartinghe	Maj. Singer took No. 3 & 4 secs. (Lt. Coombs & Fowle) to Ecole de Bienfaisance at 7pm., & then went on to Zouave wood, digging & wiring trenches on North side.	Casualty.
May 25th 1915 Vlamartinghe	Capt. Spackman took No. 1 & 2 secs. (Lt Godsell) and 100 inf. [to] continued work started on previous night at Zouave wood, digging & wiring trenches on East side.	23711 a/Lce. Cpl. Chowns. wounded by stray bullet on Menin road while returning from work.

Instructions regarding War Diaries and Intelligence Summaries are contained in F. S. Regs., Part II. and the Staff Manual respectively. Title pages will be prepared in manuscript.

WAR DIARY
or
INTELLIGENCE SUMMARY
(Erase heading not required.)

Army Form C. 2118.

Hour, Date, Place	Summary of Events and Information	Remarks and references to Appendices
May 26th 1915 Vlamartinghe	Night. Nos 3 + 4 sects (Lt Coombs & Fowle) with 600 infantry on Zillebeke line; making overhead cover & supervising infantry deepening & widening cover & support trenches.	
May 27th 1915 Vlamartinghe	Day. Remainder of Coy. pontooning & making trestles at billets.	
	Night. No 1 + 2 sects (Lt. Hall & Godsell) on Zillebeke line with 600 cavalry. Widening support trenches, digging new communication trenches & new lengths of fire and cover trench on right.	
	Day. Practising pontooning with remainder of Coy.	
May 28th 1915	Night. Nos 3 + 4 sects (Lt. Coombs & Fowle) on Zillebeke line with 600 infantry. Continued overhead cover in cover trenches, & widening support trenches.	
	Major Sniger took over duties of CRE Cav. Corps from Major Sandys RE.	

1247 W 3299 200,000 (E) 8/14 J.B.C. & A. Forms/C. 2118/11.

Army Form C. 2118.

WAR DIARY
or
INTELLIGENCE SUMMARY
(Erase heading not required.)

Instructions regarding War Diaries and Intelligence Summaries are contained in F. S. Regs., Part II. and the Staff Manual respectively. Title pages will be prepared in manuscript.

Hour, Date, Place	Summary of Events and Information	Remarks and references to Appendices
May 29th 1915. Vlamartinghe	Night. No 1 & 2 sects. (Lt. Hall & Godsell) on Zillebeke line, with 200 infantry who should have arrived at 9 pm., but did arrive at 11.30 pm.; continued work on [illegible] overhead cover, & dug new communication trench to Tuileries and deepened & widened the others. and demolished house on Zillebeke road.	
May 30th 1915 Vlamartinghe.	Preparing to move to Armentières on following day.	
May 31st 1915.	Left Vlamartinghe at 9 am. and marched to DRANOUTRE, where the company was billeted for the night in a farm, en route to ARMENTIÈRES	

27th Division

121/5871

17th Field Coy: RE

Vol XI 1—30.6.15.

Instructions re[illegible] War Diaries and Intelligence Summaries a[illegible]tained in F. S. Regs., Part II. and the Staff Manual respectively. Title pages will be prepared in manuscript.

WAR DIARY
or
INTELLIGENCE SUMMARY
(Erase heading not required.)

Army Form C. 2118.

Hour, Date, Place	Summary of Events and Information	Remarks and references to Appendices
	Confidential War Diary of 17th Field Company R.E. from June 1st 1915 to June 30th 1915 P.G. Spackman Capt R.E. for O.C. 17th Coy R.E.	 J.M. Wallinson[illegible] CRE 27th D.

1247 W 3299 200,000 (E) 8/14 J.B.C. & A. Forms/C. 2118/11.

Army Form C. 2118.

Instructions regarding War Diaries and Intelligence Summaries are contained in F. S. Regs., Part II. and the Staff Manual respectively. Title pages will be prepared in manuscript.

WAR DIARY
or
INTELLIGENCE SUMMARY.
(Erase heading not required.)

Hour, Date, Place	Summary of Events and Information	Remarks and references to Appendices
June 1st 1915.	The company left billets near Dranoutre at 5.55 am, where it had stayed the night on its way from Ypres, and arrived at Armentières at 10 a.m., via Bailleul: it was then billeted in the Lunatic Asylum, on the East of Armentières.	
June 2nd 1915. Armentieres	Drill for whole company in morning. No work as 80 & 81 Brigades had not taken over their trenches.	
June 3rd 1915. Armentieres.	Major Singer, with Capt Spackman & Lt Godsell went round 81 Brig. trenches at 6 am. Company as on 2nd.	
June 4th 1915. Armentieres.	Maj Singer, with Lt Fowle & Coombs went round 80 Brig. trenches; Lt Hall & Godsell went round remainder of 81 Brig. trenches. Company as on 2nd. Capt. Spackman inspected bridges for demolition of the R. Lys.	

(9 29 6) W4141—463 100,000 9/14 H W V Forms/C. 2118/10

Army Form C. 2118.

Instructions regarding War Diaries and Intelligence Summaries are contained in F. S. Regs., Part II. and the Staff Manual respectively. Title pages will be prepared in manuscript.

WAR DIARY
or
INTELLIGENCE SUMMARY.
(Erase heading not required.)

Hour, Date, Place	Summary of Events and Information	Remarks and references to Appendices
June 5th 1915 Armentieres.	Company - as on 2nd.	
June 6th 1915.	Day. No. 3 & 4 sects (Lt. Coombs) revetting & improving new support line in 80 Brig. sector. No 1 & 2 sects (Lt. Godsell) do. in 81st Brig sector.	
	Night. Lts. Fowle & Hall supervising infantry digging new support line in 80 & 81 Brig. sectors respectively.	
June 7th 1915.	Day No. 1 sects. (Lt. ~~Godsell~~ ~~Coombs~~ Hall) & ~~8~~ 40 civilians - revetting step & sandbagging support line between Ferme de Biez & Orchard. (81 Brig) No 4 sect (Lt. Fowle) & 40 civilians, as above, to left of Pont Ballot farm.	
	Night. No 2 sect (Lt Godsell) making dug-outs to left of Orchard. Lt. ~~Coombs~~ Fowle supervising infantry in new trench near Pont Ballot	

(9 29 6) W 4141—463 100,000 9/14 H W V Forms/C. 2118/10

Instructions regarding War Diaries and Intelligence Summaries are contained in F. S. Regs., Part II. and the Staff Manual respectively. Title pages will be prepared in manuscript.

WAR DIARY
or
INTELLIGENCE SUMMARY.
(Erase heading not required.)

Army Form C. 2118.

Hour, Date, Place	Summary of Events and Information	Remarks and references to Appendices
June 8th 1915 Armentières.	Day Nos 1, 2 + 3/4 sects (Lt. Hall & Fowle) continuing work on new support line (3am – 12 noon).	
	Night Lt Godsell + Coombs superintending infantry digging new support line.	
June 9th 1915 Armentières	Day. No 2 sect. (Lt Godsell) revetting, putting in new dug-outs, + sandbagging support line with inf. + 40 civilians. (81 Brig.)	
	No 3 sect (Lt. Coombs) as above in 80 Brig. sector.	
	Remainder making frames for dug-outs	
June 10th 1915 Armentières	Night	
	Day Making dug-out frames &c.	
	Night No 3 sect (Lt Coombs) wiring Orchard at Pont Ballot.	
	No 2. sect (Lt. Godsell) dug + wired support point ("The FORT") to left of orchard in 81 Brig sector.	

(9 29 6) W 4141—463 100,000 9/14 H W V Forms/C. 2118/10

Instructions regarding War Diaries and Intelligence Summaries are contained in F. S. Regs., Part II. and the Staff Manual respectively. Title pages will be prepared in manuscript.

WAR DIARY
or
INTELLIGENCE SUMMARY.
(Erase heading not required.)

Army Form C. 2118.

Hour, Date, Place	Summary of Events and Information	Remarks and references to Appendices
June 11th 1915 Armentieres	Day. No 2 sect. (Lt. Godsell) improving support line (81 Brig.) No 4 sect (Lt. Fowle) do (80 Brig.)	
	Night. No 1 sect (Lt Hall), with 1 sect of 69th Coy. RE, continued work on the FORT.	
	The 69th Coy. RE (Maj. Knox) were attached to this Coy for one week, for instruction.	
June 12th 1915 Armentieres	Day. Nos 2 & 3 sects (Lt. Godsell & Coombs) continued work on their support line in their respective sectors (81 & 80 Brigs), with 2 sects of the 69 Coy.	
	Night. No 4 sect (Lt Fowle) with 1 sect of 69 Coy, on support trenches & MG emplacements at Pont Ballot.	
	Dug-outs at Lunatic asylum started with Inf working party.	

(9 29 6) W4141—463 100,000 9/14 H W V Forms/C. 2118/10

Instructions regarding War Diaries and Intelligence Summaries are contained in F. S. Regs., Part II. and the Staff Manual respectively. Title pages will be prepared in manuscript.

WAR DIARY
or
INTELLIGENCE SUMMARY.
(Erase heading not required.)

Army Form C. 2118.

Hour, Date, Place	Summary of Events and Information	Remarks and references to Appendices
June 13th 1915.	Church parade 11 a.m. Ecole Professionale.	
	Night. * No 2 sect. (Lt Godsell) continued work on the "FORT". No 3 sect. (Lt. Coombs) New support trench near Bn Hdqrs begun with inf., continued wiring orchard.	
	* each with 1 sect. of 69th Coy.	
June 14th 1915.	Day. No 1 ~~sectn~~ (Lt Hall) with 50 inf. & civilians, continued improving support line to left (with 1 sect of 69 Coy).	
	No 4 sect. (Lt Fowle) with 1 sect of 69 Coy, improving support point at Pont Ballot, inf digging dug-out recesses.	
	The 69th Coy ceased being attached to this Coy. as they were to move on the 15th.	

Army Form C. 2118.

Instructions regarding War Diaries and Intelligence Summaries are contained in F. S. Regs., Part II. and the Staff Manual respectively. Title pages will be prepared in manuscript.

WAR DIARY
or
INTELLIGENCE SUMMARY.
(Erase heading not required.)

Hour, Date, Place	Summary of Events and Information	Remarks and references to Appendices
June 15th 1915. Armentières	Day. No. 1 + 2 sects. (Lt. Hall) Revetting firing step, + Sandbagging new support line: with civilians. No. 3 + 4 sects. (Lt. Fowle) erecting dug-outs + parados in support line — & improving support point at Pont Ballot.	
	Night. Lt. Godsell + Coombs supervising infantry on support line.	
June 16th 1915.	Day. No. 1 + 2 sects. (Lt. Hall) making dug-outs for Battn. Hdqrs. in school, + continuing support line. No. 3 + 4 sects. (Lt. Fowle) continuing support line.	2nd Lieut. CA Coombs wounded.
	Night. Lt. Godsell supervising infantry on support line to left of Lille Road. Lt. Coombs do. to Epinette road. Lieut. Coombs was wounded by stray bullet in the head while supervising infantry, + was taken back to Bailleul + underwent operation.	

(9 29 6) W4141—463 100,000 9/14 H W V Forms/C. 2118/10

Instructions regarding War Diaries and Intelligence Summaries are contained in F. S. Regs., Part II. and the Staff Manual respectively. Title pages will be prepared in manuscript.

WAR DIARY
or
INTELLIGENCE SUMMARY.
(Erase heading not required.)

Army Form C. 2118.

Hour, Date, Place	Summary of Events and Information	Remarks and references to Appendices
June 17th 1915. Armentieres	Day No. 1 & 2 secs (Lt. Hall) as on 16th.	12270 Sapr Clarke B wounded while revetting support line by stray bullet
	No. 3 & 4 secs (Lt Godsell) as on 16th	
	Night No work owing to reliefs.	
June 18th 1915.	Day No. 1 & 2 secs (Lt. Godsell) with 50 inf improving support line.	
	No. 3 & 4 secs (Capt Shackman) finished new trench to left of Pont Ballot & continued work on support line.	
	Night Lt. Hall, with 250 inf. continued digging support line to left	
	Lt. Fowle dug support point to right of L pruette road.	

(9 29 6) W 4141—463 100,000 9/14 H W V Forms/C. 2118/10

Army Form C. 2118.

Instructions regarding War Diaries and Intelligence Summaries are contained in F. S. Regs., Part II. and the Staff Manual respectively. Title pages will be prepared in manuscript.

WAR DIARY
or
INTELLIGENCE SUMMARY.
(Erase heading not required.)

Hour, Date, Place	Summary of Events and Information	Remarks and references to Appendices
June 20th 1915 (Sunday).	Day Church parade 10.5 am. Night Lt. Hall with 250 inf. continued support line to left. The 87 Coy R.E. were attached from this date for instruction	
June 21st 1915.	Day No. 1 & 2 sects. (Lt. Godsell) continued work on support line in 81 Brig. sector, with 1 sect. of the 87 Coy. No. 3 & 4 sects. as above, in 80th Brig. sector (Lt. Fowle) Night 1 sect. of 87 Coy (with Capt. Shackleman) wiring support point on Spinette road. 2nd Lieut Williams (T.C.) joined the company from the base, & took over No 3 section.	

(9 29 6) W4141—463 100,000 9/14 H W V Forms/C. 2118/10

Instructions regarding War Diaries and Intelligence Summaries are contained in F. S. Regs., Part II. and the Staff Manual respectively. Title pages will be prepared in manuscript.

WAR DIARY
or
INTELLIGENCE SUMMARY.
(*Erase heading not required.*)

Army Form C. 2118.

Hour, Date, Place	Summary of Events and Information	Remarks and references to Appendices
June 22nd 1915. Armentières.	Day No 3 & 4 sects., with 2 sects. of 87 Coy. (Lt. Fowle) continues work on the support line near L'Epinette.	13698 a/Cpl. Sinclair, T. wounded by stray bullet while supervising infantry working party.
	Remainder: dug-outs near billets & in carpenters shops.	
	Night Lt. Godsell, with 250 inf., continues support line towards Haystacks farm.	
June 23rd 1915.	Day No 1 & 2 sects. (Lt. Hall), & No 3 sect. (Lt. Fowle) continued on their respective support lines.	
	Remainder, with 150 inf., continues work on the dug outs near billets.	
	Night 1 sect. of 87 Coy. (with Capt. Sprackman) wiring support line near L'Epinette.	

Instructions regarding War Diaries and Intelligence Summaries are contained in F. S. Regs., Part II. and the Staff Manual respectively. Title pages will be prepared in manuscript.

WAR DIARY
or
INTELLIGENCE SUMMARY.
(*Erase heading not required.*)

Army Form C. 2118.

Hour, Date, Place	Summary of Events and Information	Remarks and references to Appendices
June 24th 1915. Armentieres	Day No 3 sect. (Lt. Williams with Lt. Fowle) on support points near Epinette No 7 sect (Lt. Hall) continued support line in 81 Brig. sector. Remainder on Billets near Lun. Asylum. Night. No work owing to reliefs	Mentions in Despatches Despatch of April 5th 15. published June 24-15. Major C.W. Singer DSO RE Lieut C&R Pottinger (deceased) Lieut KB Godsell. 13432 a/Sgt. Carter B. (deceased) ~~10545 a/Sgt Home~~
June 25th 1915	Day No 3 sect. (Lt. Williams) on support points near Epinette No 7 sect. (Lt Hall) as on 24th Remainder as on 24th	18802 a/Sgt. Macdonald J. ~~11757 a/Cpl. Chrystal~~ 13154 La Cpl. Vickery H. 25008 Pl Horley J. The following received certificates from the G.O.C. 27 Div. as having been recommended for distinguished service — 10545 a/Sgt Home RE. 11757 a/Cpl Chrystal J. and Lieut J. E. Fowle RE

(9 29 6) W4141—463 100,000 9/14 H W V Forms/C. 2118/10

Instructions regarding War Diaries and Intelligence Summaries are contained in F. S. Regs., Part II. and the Staff Manual respectively. Title pages will be prepared in manuscript.

WAR DIARY
or
INTELLIGENCE SUMMARY.
(Erase heading not required.)

Army Form C. 2118.

Hour, Date, Place	Summary of Events and Information	Remarks and references to Appendices
June 26th 1915. Armentières.	Morning. No 2 sect (Lt. Godsell) sandbagging parapet of support line. No 3 sect (Lt. Williams) on support points near Epinette	
	Night. Lt Hall with inf. continued support line right of 81 Brig orchard. Lt Fowle, with inf., do near Port Egal farm.	
June 27th 1915. Sunday.	Lt Godsell went on 6 days leave. Church parade in morning. Water supply reconnaissance during afternoon by Lt Fowle, Williams & Capt. Spackman.	

Army Form C. 2118.

Instructions regarding War Diaries and Intelligence Summaries are contained in F. S. Regs., Part II. and the Staff Manual respectively. Title pages will be prepared in manuscript.

WAR DIARY
or
INTELLIGENCE SUMMARY.
(*Erase heading not required.*)

Hour, Date, Place	Summary of Events and Information	Remarks and references to Appendices
June 28th 1915.	Morning. No 1 sect continued support line in front of 81 Brig. orchard.	
	No 3 sect. (Lt. Williams) as on 27th	
	Night. Lt Hall, with 150 inf, continued support line.	
	Lt. Fowle with inf. do in front of Petit Port Egate.	
June 29th 1915.	Remainder on Asylum dug-outs.	
	Morning. No 2 sect. on support line as on 28th	22583 S/2Cpl. Bland, L. wounded by stray bullet while supervising infantry.
	No 3 & 4 sects (Lt Williams) on support points at Epinette	
	Night. No 4 sect (Lt Fowle) wiring support pt. Epinette. inf. levelling parapets.	
	Lt. Hall with inf finished 81 Brig. support line.	
June 30th 1915.	Morning No 2 sect. on support line	
	No. 3 sect. (Lt. Williams) completed M.G. emplacements & dug-outs in Epinette support points.	
	Night Lt. Hall with 100 inf. deepened support line	
	Remainder on dug-outs at Asylum, preparing Rifle range	

27th Division

121/6342

17th Field Coy. R.E.

Vol XII

Army Form C. 2118.

Instructions regarding War Diaries and Intelligence Summaries are contained in F. S. Regs., Part II. and the Staff Manual respectively. Title pages will be prepared in manuscript.

WAR DIARY
or
INTELLIGENCE SUMMARY

(Erase heading not required.)

Hour, Date, Place	Summary of Events and Information	Remarks and references to Appendices
	Confidential War Diary of 17 Field Coy R.E. for period July 1st to 31st 1915 P.J. Spackman Capt R.E. for O.C. 17 Coy R.E. 2.8.15	

1247 W 3299 200,000 (E) 8/14 J.B.C. & A. Forms/C. 2118/11.

Army Form C. 2118.

Instructions regarding War Diaries and Intelligence Summaries are contained in F. S. Regs., Part II. and the Staff Manual respectively. Title pages will be prepared in manuscript.

WAR DIARY
or
~~INTELLIGENCE SUMMARY~~

(Erase heading not required.)

1

Hour, Date, Place	Summary of Events and Information	Remarks and references to Appendices
1.7.1915	Maj. Singer went on leave. Lieut Godsell & No 2 continued work in Support Line (81st Bde) [illegible] Williams & No 3 & 4 ditto in 80th Bde area. No night work.	
2.7.15	Lieut Hall & Williams & No 1.2.3 Sections continued in Support Line. No 4 made dugout frames & repaired Bde MG range. Night. Lieut Foote supervised 200 Inf. digging recesses for dugouts in support line.	
3.7.15	No 1 & 2 (Lieut Hall) finished support line in 80 Bde area. Remainder repaired rifle range & made dugout frames. No night work.	
4.7.15	C of E parade morning. Night. Lieut Hall & NCOs of No 1 supervised carrying party of [illegible] men taking dugout frames etc. to support line - also 200 Inf. digging recesses for dugouts.	
5.7.15 5 a.m.	Lieut Godsell & Williams (No 2.3.4) erecting dugout frames in support line. Night. Lieut Foote supervised carrying party of [illegible] men taking dugout materials to support line.	

1247 W 3290 200,000 (E) 8/14 J.B.C. & A. Forms/C. 2118/11.

Instructions regarding War Diaries and Intelligence Summaries are contained in F. S. Regs., Part II. and the Staff Manual respectively. Title pages will be prepared in manuscript.

WAR DIARY
or
INTELLIGENCE SUMMARY
(Erase heading not required.)

Army Form C. 2118.

2

Hour, Date, Place	Summary of Events and Information	Remarks and references to Appendices
6.7.15	Lieut Hall & Williams erecting dugouts with No 1-3-4 in Support line Night – Lieuts Godsell & Williams supervised 250 Inf digging Communication trench in 80 Bde area. Also 100 Inf. carrying materials for dugouts.	
7.7.15	Lieut Fowle & No 1-2-4 erecting dugouts in support line Night. Lieut Hall supervised 100 Inf. carrying & 100 Inf. digging communication trench.	
8.7.15	Lieut Godsell with No 2-3-4 erecting dugouts in support line. Lieut Williams went away for Bomb instruction. Night. Lieut Fowle supervised 100 Inf. from each Bde. digging dugout recesses. Capt Spackman supervised carrying party of 100 Inf.	
9.7.15	Lieut Hall with No 1-3-4 erecting dugouts in support line. Remainder making dugout frames. Night Lieut Godsell supervised 100 Inf. digging dugout recesses & 100 Inf carrying materials.	
10.7.15	Capt Spackman went on leave. Lieut Fowle & No 2.3.4 erecting dugouts in support line. No 1 Sect. drill in morning. Lieut Godsell reconnoitred drainage of CHARDS FARM. Night. Lieut Hall supervised 200 Inf. digging dugout recesses & a carrying party.	

Instructions regarding War Diaries and Intelligence Summaries are contained in F. S. Regs., Part II. and the Staff Manual respectively. Title pages will be prepared in manuscript.

WAR DIARY
or
INTELLIGENCE SUMMARY

(Erase heading not required.)

Army Form C. 2118.

3

Hour, Date, Place	Summary of Events and Information	Remarks and references to Appendices
11 7 15	Lieut Godsell with No 1.2 erecting in support line dugouts. Nos 3 & 4 made dugout frames in aft. Night Lieut ~~Williams~~ Fowle supervised Inf digging dugout recesses & also an Inf carrying party.	
12 7 15	Lieut Hall & No 1.3.4 erecting dugouts in support line. No 2 employed in workshops. Lieut Godsell took officers in Bomb instruction & Inf in barbed wiring instruction. Night Lieut Godsell supervised 100 Inf widening & deepening communication trench in 80 Bde area.	
13 7 15	Lieut Fowle & No 1.2.4 erecting dugouts in support line. No 2 workshops. Lieut Hall took officers Bomb class & Inf barbed wiring classes. Lieut Williams returned from Bomb instruction course. Night Lieut Hall supervised Inf carrying party of 100 bringing up dugout materials.	
14 7 15	Lieut Godsell & Nos 1.3.4 erecting dugouts in support line. Cpl Pelham put up [illegible] for G.O.C. dugout. No 2 workshops & drill. Lieut Fowle reconnoitred a bridge for demolition. Night. Lieut Fowle supervised an Inf carrying party.	
15 7 15	Lieut Hall & No 1.2.4 erecting dugouts in support line. No 3 drill & workshops. Night Lieut Williams supervised wiring by 80 Bde pioneers. Major Singer promoted Lieut-Col. & appointed C.R.E. 50th Divn	

1247 W 3299 200,000 (E) 8/14 J.B.C. & A. Forms/C. 2118/11.

Instructions regarding War Diaries and Intelligence Summaries are contained in F. S. Regs., Part II. and the Staff Manual respectively. Title pages will be prepared in manuscript.

WAR DIARY
or
INTELLIGENCE SUMMARY
(Erase heading not required.)

Army Form C. 2118.

4

Hour, Date, Place	Summary of Events and Information	Remarks and references to Appendices
16. 7. 1915	Lieut Fowle + No 2.3.4 on support line – No 1 in workshops. Night. Lieut Williams supervised wiring of 8th Bn. [illegible] Lieut Hall supervised Inf carrying party.	
17. 7. 15	No 2 + 3 on support line – Remainder employed in moving to new billets in morn [illegible] workshops in aft. Lieut Godsell supervised pioneers wiring at night.	
18. 7. 15	C of E parade morning – Lieut Hall supervised 30 Inf. carrying. Night. Lieut Hall supervised pioneers wiring + 100 Inf. carrying. Capt Spackman returned from leave + Lieut Fowle went on leave.	
19. 7. 15	Lieut Williams + No 1+4 on dugout roofs – Remainder moved billets to RUE MARLE Capt Spackman + Lieut Hall reconnoitred trench 59 + its support line. Night Lieut Godsell supervised 50 Inf. filling over support line dugout roofs.	
20. 7. 15.	Lieut Hall + No 2 3 sandbagging parados of support line – Revetted part of RAILWAY AVENUE – Put in cases where a communication trench comes under parapet of 60 S. No 1 + 4. trench boards in morn + making dugouts near billets in aft. Night Lieut Hall supervised 100 Inf. carrying. Lieut Williams supervised 2 pioneer wiring parties + 100 Inf. covering dugout roofs. Capt Spackman inspected all night work.	

1247 W 3299 200,000 (E) 8/14 J.B.C. & A. Forms/C. 2118/11.

Instructions regarding War Diaries and Intelligence Summaries are contained in F. S. Regs., Part II. and the Staff Manual respectively. Title pages will be prepared in manuscript.

WAR DIARY
or
INTELLIGENCE SUMMARY
(Erase heading not required.)

Army Form C. 2118.

5

Hour, Date, Place	Summary of Events and Information	Remarks and references to Appendices
21.7.15	Lieut Godsell & No4 sandbagging parados of support line – No 1-2-3 making dugouts near billets. Night Lieut Hall supervised 2 pioneer wiring parties & 50 Inf. filling in dugout parados. Capt Sparkman reconnoitred trenches 87.	
22.7.15	2 Lieut Williams & No1 sandbagging support line parados – No 2 3. in dugouts near billets – No4 workshops – Night Lieut Godsell supervised Inf carrying party of 150 men & 2 pioneer wiring parties – No 2 commenced revetment of a breastwork communication trench left of WINE Av. & erected a screen along road to ORCHARD	
23.7.15	Lieut Hall & No 3.4 digging pit props & sandbagging in the support line No1 workshops – Night 2 Lieut Williams & No1 continued Breastwork C.T. revetment & screen – supervised 50 Inf filling Bw C.T.× 100 Inf filling roofs & parados in support line – 50 Inf	× Bw C.T = Breastwork Communication Trench.
24.7.15	Carrying Lieut Godsell & No 2 3 sandbagging revetting dugout steps – No4 workshops – No1 all dugout frames & sharpened pickets. Major Gracey arrived to take over Coy – Night Lieut Hall & No4 continued revetting Bw C.T.× & erecting screen – supervised 200 Inf filling in Bw C.T.× & 2 pioneer parties wiring. Capt Sparkman sited M.G. emplacements with M.G. officer	

Instructions regarding War Diaries and Intelligence Summaries are contained in F. S. Regs., Part II. and the Staff Manual respectively. Title pages will be prepared in manuscript.

WAR DIARY
or
INTELLIGENCE SUMMARY
(Erase heading not required.)

Army Form C. 2118.

6.

Hour, Date, Place	Summary of Events and Information	Remarks and references to Appendices
25 7 1915	C of E parade morning. 2 Lieut Williams & 30 Inf excavated G.O.Cs dugout. Lieut Williams went to see CRE re an electrification scheme in aft.	
	Night. Lieut Godsell & No 2 continued on Bn C.T. & screen. Supervised 2 wiring parties & 200 Inf filling Bn C.T.	
26. 7 1915	Lieut Hall & No 1 & commenced framework of G.O.Cs dugout & a dugout for a F.O.O. No 3 sandbagging parados of support line	
	No 4 workshops & commenced a M.G range at L'ARMEE.	
	Night. Lieut Fowle started 250 Inf filling Bn C.T. 2 Lieut Williams & No 4 continued revetting Bn C.T. & erecting screen. Supervised 50 Inf filling parados of support line dugouts.	
27 7 15	Lieut Godsell & Nos 1 & 2 sandbagging parados of support line & ~~completed the~~ continued erection of framework of G.O.Cs dugout & completed F.O.O. dugout.	
	No 3 constructing M.G range & workshops.	
	2 Lieut Williams commenced investigation for electrical scheme. No 4 workshops in aft.	
	Night. Lieut Fowle & No 3 (part) erecting screen & supervised 150 Inf filling Bn C.T. & 2 pioneer parties wiring.	
28 7 15	Lieut Hall & No 2 continued framework of G.O.Cs dugout. & No 4 sandbagging support line. Supervised 30 Inf laying trench boards. No 1 workshops.	
	2 Lieut Williams continued electrical investigations.	
	Capt. Stockman & Lieut Hall reconnoitred support line of trench 59.	

1247 W 3299 200,000 (E) 8/14 J.B.C. & A. Forms/C. 2118/11.

Instructions regarding War Diaries and Intelligence Summaries are contained in F. S. Regs., Part II. and the Staff Manual respectively. Title pages will be prepared in manuscript.

WAR DIARY
or
INTELLIGENCE SUMMARY
(Erase heading not required.)

Army Form C. 2118.

7

Hour, Date, Place	Summary of Events and Information	Remarks and references to Appendices
28.7.15 (Cont.)	night Lieut Godsell & No 1 continued revetting Bn C.T. and erecting screen. Supervised 250 Inf. filling Bn C.T. 2 wiring parties – 250 Inf. filling roofs of dugouts of support line dugouts.	
29.7.15.	Lieut Fowle & No 2 continued erecting framework of G.O.C. dugout and [illegible] frames of support line. Supervised 20 Inf. laying floor boards. Remainder workshops & washing gravel for concrete. 2 Lieut Williams continued electrical investigations.	
	night 2 Lieut Williams & No 3 continued revetting Bn C.T. & erecting screen. Supervised 2 wiring parties & 200 Inf. filling Bn C.T.	
30.7.15	Lieut Godsell & No 2 erected dugouts in S95 & supervised 20 Inf. laying floorboards. Lieut Hall & two reliefs of No 4 commenced concreting roof of G.O.C. dugout.	
	night Lieut Fowle & No 3 revetted Bn C.T. & supervised 200 Inf filling it; also 2 wiring [illegible]. Major Godsell, Lieut [illegible] Rowe [illegible] on a Court Martial.	
31.7.15	Lieut Hall & half No 1 continued concreting roof of G.O.C.'s dugout. Lieut Godsell & details continued erecting dugouts in S95. Remainder employed in workshops. No night work –	

G. Hall.
Lieut RE (SR).
1/8/15.

27th Division

121/6743

17th Field Coy R.E.

Vol XIII

August 15

Army Form C. 2118.

WAR DIARY
or
~~INTELLIGENCE SUMMARY.~~

(Erase heading not required.)

Instructions regarding War Diaries and Intelligence Summaries are contained in F. S. Regs., Part II. and the Staff Manual respectively. Title pages will be prepared in manuscript.

Hour, Date, Place	Summary of Events and Information	Remarks and references to Appendices
	Confidential War Diary of 17th Field Company R.E. for period Aug. 1st to 31st 1915. J. Gracey. Major R.E. Comdg. 17 Field Coy. R.E. 2/9/15	[illegible] Capt [illegible] for CRE 21 [illegible]

(73989) W4141—463. 400,000. 9/14. H.&J.Ltd. Forms/C. 2118/10.

Instructions regarding War Diaries and Intelligence Summaries are contained in F. S. Regs., Part II. and the Staff Manual respectively. Title pages will be prepared in manuscript.

WAR DIARY
or
INTELLIGENCE SUMMARY.

(Erase heading not required.)

Army Form C. 2118.

1.

Hour, Date, Place		Summary of Events and Information	Remarks and references to Appendices
August. 1915. Armentiers.	1st	Lieut. Fowle took Church Parade.	
		Night. Lieut. Godsell & No 2 Section continued revetting Bw. C.T. Superintended pioneer wiring parties & 200 Infantry filling in Bw. C.T.	Reference. Bw. C.T = Breastwork Communication Trench.
	2nd	Lieut. Hall & No1. Sect. continued on G.O.C's dugout. Concrete roof completed, floors & drains commenced.	
		Lieut. Williams & No3. Sect. erected dugouts in 59S.	
		Remainder in workshops.	
		Night. Lieut. Fowle laid out direction of Bw. C.T. and light railway.	
	3rd	Lieut. Hall & No1 continued on G.O.C's dugout.	
		Lieut Godsell & No2 + 1 sect. of 84th Fd Coy putting in dugouts in 59S.	
		Night. Lieut. Fowle superintended a carrying party. Lieut Williams & No3. revetting Bw. C.T. one sect. 84th Fd Coy also employed. 300 Inf. filling Bw. C.T.	
	4th	Major Gracey returned from ROUEN.	
		Lieut. Godsell & No2 + 1 sect. 84th Coy — dugouts & parados in 59S.	
		Lieut Hall & No1. Continued on G.O.C's dugout & put in the foundations for a reinforced Concrete M.G. Emplacement in 63.	
		Remainder in workshops & breaking slag for concrete	

Instructions regarding War Diaries and Intelligence Summaries are contained in F. S. Regs., Part II. and the Staff Manual respectively. Title pages will be prepared in manuscript.

WAR DIARY
or
INTELLIGENCE SUMMARY.
(Erase heading not required.)

Army Form C. 2118.

2

Hour, Date, Place	Summary of Events and Information	Remarks and references to Appendices
4th	night. Lieut Godsell started 100 Inf. filling parados of 59S.	
	Lieut Fowle superintended 3 pioneer parties wiring COWGATE AVENUE - 200 Inf. on Bn. C.T.	
5th	Lieut Hall & No1 erected wall of Concrete M.G. Emplacement in 63 - & continued on G.O.C's dugout.	
	Lieut Godsell Nos 2 & 4 & two sections of the 84th Fd. Coy put in dugouts in 59S - reconstructed 64S - 30 Inf remodelling trench in front of Orchard.	
	night. Lieut Williams superintended 3 pioneer parties wiring COWGATE AVENUE - 100 Inf filling parados of support line - 50 Inf. making firing steps in RAILWAY AVENUE	
6th	Lieut Hall & No1 G.O.C's dugout - & prepared site for another M.G. Emplacement.	
	Lieut Godsell No2 & part No3 + two sections of the 84th Fd. Coy. remodelling Orchard trench - improving 59S & converted a Bn. C.T. behind RUE DE BOIS into fire trench.	
	Aft. Lieut Williams superintended 2 Inf. parties putting in firing bays in WINE and RAILWAY AVENUES.	
	night. Lieut. Fowle & No4 + one section of 84th Fd. Coy revetting Bn. C.T. - superintended 3 pioneer parties wiring COWGATE AVENUE - 100 Inf. filling	

Instructions regarding War Diaries and Intelligence Summaries are contained in F. S. Regs., Part II. and the Staff Manual respectively. Title pages will be prepared in manuscript.

WAR DIARY
or
INTELLIGENCE SUMMARY.
(Erase heading not required.)

Army Form C. 2118.

3.

Hour, Date, Place	Summary of Events and Information	Remarks and references to Appendices
	parapet & parados of 595. 150 inf dug new trench behind RUE DE BOIS – 50 inf on G.O.C's dugout & 30 inf carrying stores.	
7th.	Lieut Hall & No1. continued on 2 R. Concrete M.G. Emplacements. 50 inf carrying materials.	
	Lieut Godsell & No2 + two sections of the 56th Fd Coy remodelling ORCHARD trench and Bw. behind RUE DE BOIS – 50 inf digging ORCHARD trench.	
	Night Lieuts Fowle & Williams superintended 3 pioneer parties wiring ORCHARD – 100 inf. filling parapet & parados of 595 – 100 inf. 2nd relief on trench behind RUE DE BOIS. No3 Sect + 1 sect. of 56th Fd Coy revetting Bw. C.T. + 200 inf. filling it.	
	Lieut Hall and ½ No1 Sect. spent on Reinforced Concrete roof to M.G. Emplacement in 63.	
8th.	Lieut Godsell took Church parade – No1 Sect. were inoculated –	
	Night. Lieut. Godsell & No2. revetting Bw. C.T. – made a bridge over a stream & repaired another. Sandbagging parapet of 595 – 200 inf. on Bw. C.T. – 50 inf. on G.O.C's dugout – 100 inf. on 595 + 25 inf. filling sandbags –	

Instructions regarding War Diaries and Intelligence Summaries are contained in F. S. Regs., Part II. and the Staff Manual respectively. Title pages will be prepared in manuscript.

WAR DIARY
or
INTELLIGENCE SUMMARY.
(Erase heading not required.)

Army Form C. 2118.

4.

Hour, Date, Place	Summary of Events and Information	Remarks and references to Appendices
9th	Lieut Hall & 1/2 No 1 + 1/2 sect. of 84th Fd Coy continued on Concrete M.G. Emplacements – 40 Inf. carrying. Lieut Fowle & No 4 remodelled ORCHARD trench & 64 S – Put dugouts in 64 S – M.G. Emplacement & remodelled trench in front of 64 S – 1 Sect. of 84th Fd Coy remodelling Bw. behind RUE DE BOIS. another sect. of 84th Coy improving 61 S. Night. Lieut Williams & pioneer parties wiring ORCHARD & WINE ST – No 3 Sect. revetted Bw CT.	
10th	Lieut Fowle & 1/2 No 4. completed 64 S – 1 Sect. of 84th Coy continued on trench behind RUE DE BOIS – 1/2 sect. of 84th Coy + 10 Inf. on parados of 59 S – 1/2 Sect 84th parados to trench behind RUE DE BOIS – Nos 1 & 1/2 No 4 breaking stone for concrete in morning & No 1 + 3. ditto in aft. Capt. Shackman took Inf. officers round trenches to show them work to be done for next week. (Inf. in future to work on their own). Night. Lieut Godsell & No 2 revetting Bw CT. + 3 pioneer parties wiring Lieut Campion + 20 sappers arrived to lay light railway.	

Army Form C. 2118.

Instructions regarding War Diaries and Intelligence Summaries are contained in F. S. Regs., Part II. and the Staff Manual respectively. Title pages will be prepared in manuscript.

WAR DIARY
or
INTELLIGENCE SUMMARY.
(Erase heading not required.)

5.

Hour, Date, Place	Summary of Events and Information	Remarks and references to Appendices
11th	Lieut Fowle & No 4 + 2 Sects of the 84th Fd Coy - dugouts in 61 S - remodling 62 S - revetted firing steps in trench behind RUE DE BOIS. Sandbagged parados of 59 S - 2 reliefs of 30 Inf. digging -	
	Lieut Hall & No 1 continued on 2 R. Concrete M.G. Emplacements. 60 Inf. carrying materials -	
	Lieut Godsell appointed Staff officer to CE IIIrd Corps.	
	night. Lieut Williams & No 3. revetting Bn. CT - 3 wiring parties -	
12th	Lieut Fowle + ½ No 4 + 2 sections of 84th Fd Coy & 2 reliefs of 30 Inf - dugouts in RUE DE BOIS support trench & Sandbagged parados of trench to left of above - Laid floor boards sapped a trench into RAILWAY AVENUE. Sandbagged 59 S.	
	Lt Hall & No 1. Reinforced Concrete M.G. Emplacement in 62 -	
	night. Lieut Hall & No 2 revetted Bn. CT. + 2 wiring parties. Capt Sparkman & Lieut Hall blew up rails of the LILLE - ARMENTIERS RY	
13th	Lieut Fowle & Nos 1 & 4 + 2 Sects of 84th Coy & 2 reliefs of 30 Inf. Parados of 61 S - Completed dugouts in support line - RUE DE BOIS - Continued on trench behind trench right of RY + Communication trench by RY - M.G. Emplacement in RY behind RUE DE BOIS - laying trench boards -	

Instructions regarding War Diaries and Intelligence Summaries are contained in F. S. Regs., Part II. and the Staff Manual respectively. Title pages will be prepared in manuscript.

WAR DIARY
or
INTELLIGENCE SUMMARY.
(Erase heading not required.)

Army Form C. 2118.

6.

Hour, Date, Place	Summary of Events and Information	Remarks and references to Appendices
	Night. 2/Lieut. Williams & No 3 revetting Pow CT – 3 pioneer parties wiring WINE AVENUE.	
14th	Lt Hall & No 1. R. Converts roof to M.G. Emplacement in 62 Lt Fowle & No 4 – Improving 595 & dugouts in new support line – 2 reliefs 30 inf. filling sandbags – Laid charges for demolition of 2 houses behind RUE DE BOIS.	
	Night. Capt. Spackman & Lieut Fowle blew up houses mentioned above. 2/Lieut. Williams – & No 3. sandbagging parapet of 59S – 2 pioneer parties wiring WINE AVENUE	
15th	Night. Lieut Hall & No 1 – sandbagged parapet of 59S – & roof of G.O.C.s dugouts – 1 pioneer party wiring WINE AVENUE & 1 party revetting trench round RAILWAY FARM.	
16th	Lieut Fowle & No 2 + 3 + 2 reliefs of 50 inf. sandbagging & putting in dugouts in trench behind RUE DE BOIS – Improving 59S – Parados to trench in front of S.64. Improving ORCHARD trench – revetted firing steps in RAILWAY AVENUE – No 1. dugouts near billets.	
	Night. 2/Lt. Williams supervised a carrying party.	

(73989) W4141—463. 400,000. 9/14. H.&J.Ltd. Forms/C. 2118/10.

Army Form C. 2118.

WAR DIARY
or
INTELLIGENCE SUMMARY.
(Erase heading not required.)

7

Instructions regarding War Diaries and Intelligence Summaries are contained in F. S. Regs., Part II. and the Staff Manual respectively. Title pages will be prepared in manuscript.

Hour, Date, Place	Summary of Events and Information	Remarks and references to Appendices
17th	Lieut Fowle No 1+4 + 2 reliefs of 30 Inf. dugouts in RUE DE BOIS support line – improving 59S & trenches round RAILWAY FARM – improved trench in front of 64S.	
	night. Lieut Hall & No 3. Sandbagged parapet of 59S. Laid out line for a C.T. from 59S to BOIS GRENIER RD. 3 pioneer parties completed wiring WINE AVENUE & commenced on HAYSTACK AV.	
18th	Lieut Fowle No 2+4 + 2 reliefs of 50 Inf. improving 59S and trenches round RAILWAY FARM – filling paradoes of 60S & 64S. 30 Inf. putting in firing steps in HAYSTACK AVENUE	
	Lieut. Hall instructed attached Inf. officers in sandbag revetment & Barbed wire entanglements.	
	night. " Lt Williams & No 1 revetted Bois C.T. & 3 pioneer parties wiring HAYSTACK AVENUE	
19th	" Lieut Barton joined the Company.	
	Lieut Fowle & No 2+3 made a bridge over the COURANTE CHAPPELLE in 60S & 64S – 4 parties of improved 59S – 2 reliefs of 50 Inf. in Communication Trenches. 30 Inf. making firing steps in	
	night. Lieut Hall & No 4 revetted Bois C.T. – 3 pioneer parties wiring HAYSTACK AVENUE.	
	Lieut Hall instructed Inf. officers in Barbed Wire Entanglements.	

Instructions regarding War Diaries and Intelligence Summaries are contained in F.S. Regs., Part II. and the Staff Manual respectively. Title pages will be prepared in manuscript.

WAR DIARY
or
INTELLIGENCE SUMMARY.
(Erase heading not required.)

Army Form C. 2118.

8.

Hour, Date, Place	Summary of Events and Information	Remarks and references to Appendices
20th	Lieut Fowle & 2/Lt Barton & No2 + 60 Inf. improving 595 - 635. and RAILWAY AVENUE - 4 parties of 30 infantry on firing steps in communication trenches.	
	Lieut Hall instructed Inf officers in wire netting revetment.	
	Night.	
	2/Lieut Williams & No3. revetted Bn. C.T. - 2 parties wiring HAYSTACK AVENUE & 1 party WINE AVENUE.	
21st	Lieut Fowle & 2/Lieut Barton & No2. improved 595 - No4 revetted firing steps in 6 & 5 - [illegible] carrying & laying trench boards -	
	Lieut Hall instructed Inf officers in constructing dugouts.	
	Night.	
	Lieut Hall 3 parties completed wiring HAYSTACK AVENUE up to support line - 150 Inf on new C.T. right of railway - working parties on G.O.C.s dugouts & Bn. C.T.	
22nd	2/Lieut Williams took C. of E. parade -	
	Night.	
	Lieut Fowle & 2/Lieut Barton supervised 3 parties wiring RAILWAY AVENUE - No4 Sect. laying pit props on roof of G.O.C.s dugout - 150 Inf on new C.T.	
23rd	Lieut Hall & No 1 & 3. Improved 595 - made an M.G. emplacement in 595 - trench boards left of 595 & in C.T. by railway. Revetted firing steps in 6 & 5 - Concrete floor to M.G. emplacement in 62 - 30 Inf carrying materials.	

Instructions regarding War Diaries and Intelligence Summaries are contained in F. S. Regs., Part II. and the Staff Manual respectively. Title pages will be prepared in manuscript.

WAR DIARY
or
INTELLIGENCE SUMMARY.
(Erase heading not required.)

Army Form C. 2118.

9.

Hour, Date, Place	Summary of Events and Information	Remarks and references to Appendices
	Lieut Foole instructed Inf officers in extending working parties.	
	Night.	
	11 Lieut Williams & No 2 carried materials up to the trenches	
24th.	Lieut Hall & No. 1 & 3 - firing steps in 59S - improved M.G. Emplacement by RAILWAY FARM & laid trench boards round this farm. Revetted top of RAILWAY AVENUE - revetted firing steps in 64 S. Commenced two shelters for M. Gunners in 64 & 65.	
	11 Lieut Barton instructed Inf. officers in demolitions.	
	Major Gracy went round trenches with C.R.E.	
	Night.	
	11 Lt. Barton & No 2 revetted Bw. C.T. - 3 parties wiring RAILWAY AVENUE.	
25th.	11 Lieut Williams & No 3 + 15 Inf. revetted 59S - revetted WILLOW AVENUE & put firing bays in SALOP AVENUE.	
	Lieut Hall & No 1 continued on 2 shelters for M. Gunners & commenced 3 more. 30 Inf. improving BRICK AVENUE.	
	30 Inf. carrying - 30 Inf. excavating holes for shelters.	
	Lieut Foole instructed Inf. officers in strength of materials.	
	Night.	
	Lieut Foole & No 4. Revetted Bw. C.T. & laid sand bags & pit props on G.O.C's dugout. Infantry at Bw C.T.	
26th.	Lieut Hall continued on M.G. shelters - 30 Inf. improving ~~Brick~~ BRICK STREET - 30 Inf. carrying.	
	11 Lieut Williams & No 3 revetted 59S, & WILLOW AVENUE & put firing steps in SALOP AVENUE.	

Instructions regarding War Diaries and Intelligence Summaries are contained in F. S. Regs., Part II. and the Staff Manual respectively. Title pages will be prepared in manuscript.

WAR DIARY
or
INTELLIGENCE SUMMARY.
(*Erase heading not required.*)

Army Form C. 2118.

10.

Hour, Date, Place	Summary of Events and Information	Remarks and references to Appendices
	night. 2/Lieut Barton & No 2 revetted Bw. C.T. – 3 parties wiring SALOP AVENUE – 50 Inf. in RUE DE BOIS AVENUE – 50 Inf. in G.O.C. dugout.	
27th	2/Lieut Williams & No 3. revetted WILLOW AVENUE – Sandbagged S.9.S. – 2 reliefs of 30 Inf firing steps in RAILWAY and SALOP AVENUES –	
	Lieut Hall & No 1. Completed 2 shelters for M. Gunners, continued on another & started 2 more – 30 Inf. carrying – 40 Inf firing steps in WINE AVENUE – 6 Inf. improving BRICK STREET –	
	night Lieut Fowle & No 4. revetted Bw. C.T. & supervised Infantry.	
28th	2/Lieut Williams & No 3 – (Same as on 27th)	29th
	Lieut Hall & No 1. Continued on 3 M.G. shelters. 80 Inf. completed firing steps in WINE AVENUE.	No 27907 Sergt Major Armour killed.
	night. 2/Lieut Barton & No 2 revetted Bw. C.T. 2 pioneer parties wiring HAYSTACK AVENUE & 1 wiring SALOP AVENUE.	No 25745 Sapper Ford. wounded by shell near billets.
29th	2/Lieut Williams took C. of E. Parade.	

Instructions regarding War Diaries and Intelligence Summaries are contained in F. S. Regs., Part II. and the Staff Manual respectively. Title pages will be prepared in manuscript.

WAR DIARY
or
INTELLIGENCE SUMMARY.
(Erase heading not required.)

Army Form C. 2118.

Hour, Date, Place	Summary of Events and Information	Remarks and references to Appendices
August 30th 1915. Rue Marle Armentieres.	Day No 1 & 4 sects. (Lieut. Fowle) continued work on machine gun emplacements & new support trenches behind Rue de Bois. Night. No work owing to 82nd Brigade relieving 80th Brigade in the left sector.	
Aug. 31st 1915. Rue Marle Armentieres.	Day No 1 & 4 sects. (Lieut. Fowle) as on 30th. Night. No 3 sect. (Lieut. Williams) started revetting Wellington Avenue with hurdles, & supervised infantry on breastwork commun. trench & Rue de Bois.	

(73989) W4141—463. 400,000. 9/14. H.&J.Ltd. Forms/C. 2118/10.

27th Division

121
7049

17th Field Coy RE

Vol XIV

Sep. 15

Instructions regarding War Diaries and Intelligence Summaries are contained in F. S. Regs., Part II. and the Staff Manual respectively. Title pages will be prepared in manuscript.

Army Form C. 2118.

WAR DIARY
or
INTELLIGENCE SUMMARY.
(Erase heading not required.)

Hour, Date, Place	Summary of Events and Information	Remarks and references to Appendices
	Confidential War Diary of 17 Field Coy. R.E. for period 1st Sept to 30th Sept 1915. Spacey. Major R.E. Comdg. 17 Field Company R.E.	HEADQUARTERS * 5-OCT. 1915 197 * 27th DIVISIONAL ENGINEERS

[signature] Lt. Col. R.E.
C.R.E. 24th Division
5/10/15.

(73989) W4141—463. 400,000. 9/14. H.&J.Ltd. Forms/C. 2118/10.

Instructions regarding War Diaries and Intelligence Summaries are contained in F. S. Regs., Part II. and the Staff Manual respectively. Title pages will be prepared in manuscript.

WAR DIARY
or
INTELLIGENCE SUMMARY.
(Erase heading not required.)

Army Form C. 2118.

Hour, Date, Place	Summary of Events and Information	Remarks and references to Appendices
Billets at Rue Marle Armentieres	Day	
1. 9. 15	No 1 + 4 sects (Lieut Fowle) continued work on M.G. shelters, Cow lane (converting into fire trench) and revetting trenches behind Rue de Bois.	
	Night. No 2 sect (2 Lieut Barton) revetting Wellington Avenue with hurdles & supervising infantry, 400 on Breastwork Avenue, pioneers wiring trenches behind Rue de Bois	
2. 9. 15	Day No 3 sect (2 Lt Williams) left on detachment for making bombs at St Venant	
	Day work as on 1st	
	Night No 2 sect. (2 Lt Barton) continued work on Wellington Avenue, & supervised 400 inf. on Breastwork Avenue.	

(73989) W4141—463. 400,000. 9/14. H.&J.Ltd. Forms/C. 2118/10.

Army Form C. 2118.

Instructions regarding War Diaries and Intelligence Summaries are contained in F. S. Regs., Part II. and the Staff Manual respectively. Title pages will be prepared in manuscript.

WAR DIARY
or
INTELLIGENCE SUMMARY.

(Erase heading not required.)

Hour, Date, Place	Summary of Events and Information	Remarks and references to Appendices
Billets at Rue Marle Armentieres 3.9.15.	Day No 1 & 4 sects. (Lt. Fowle) as on 1st. Night Lieut Barton (No 2 sect.) revetting Wellington Av. with hurdles, & supervised 400 inf. on Breastwork Av. and pioneers wiring Haystack Avenue.	
4.9.15.	Day No 4 sect. (Lt. Fowle) continued work as on 1st, No 1 sect (Lt. Hall) making Machine Gun Shelters Night work was cancelled owing to rain.	
5.9.15.	Sunday: Bathing parade 10.30 am. (Lieut Fowle). Night 2/Lt. Barton No 2 sect. revetting Breastwork Av. & erecting screen at Chapelle d'Armentieres & supervising 150 inf. on Breastwork Av. & pioneers wiring Cowgate Avenue.	

Instructions regarding War Diaries and Intelligence Summaries are contained in F. S. Regs., Part II. and the Staff Manual respectively. Title pages will be prepared in manuscript.

WAR DIARY
or
INTELLIGENCE SUMMARY.
(Erase heading not required.)

Army Form C. 2118.

Hour, Date, Place	Summary of Events and Information	Remarks and references to Appendices
Billets at Rue Marle Armentieres		
6. 9. 15.	Day — No 4 sect (Lt. Fowle) continued work on Cowlane + Machine Gun emplacements.	
	Night — Work was cancelled owing to rain.	
7. 9. 15.	Day — Lt. Fowle with No 1 + 4 sects as on 6th	
	Night — No 2 sect (2Lt. Barker) putting up hurdle revetments on Wellington Avenue, making look out post in No 59 trench; pioneers wiring Cowgate Avenue + erecting screen for Chapelle d'Armentieres road.	

(73989) W4141—463. 400,000. 9/14. H.&J.Ltd. Forms/C. 2118/10.

Instructions regarding War Diaries and Intelligence Summaries are contained in F. S. Regs., Part II. and the Staff Manual respectively. Title pages will be prepared in manuscript.

WAR DIARY
or
INTELLIGENCE SUMMARY.
(Erase heading not required.)

Army Form C. 2118.

1

Hour, Date, Place	Summary of Events and Information	Remarks and references to Appendices
8. 9. 1915	Lt Hall, No 1 Section & 2 reliefs of 110 Inf. continued on 3 Shelters for M. Gunners & filled up the roofs of 6 others. Filling parados of COWLANE – Cleared drains of COWGATE and WINE AVENUES and re-revetted firing steps of support line between COWGATE AV. and LILLE RD.	
	Remainder in workshops –	
	5 Inf. officers of 80th Bde attached for instruction –	
	Night.	
	Lt Fowle & No 4 revetted BREASTWORK AV. – 300 Inf. filling it & pioneers laying floorboards in it – ½ No 2 Section put look out posts in trench 63 –	
9-9-15.	Lt Hall & No 1 completed an M.G. Shelter & continued on 2 others – 2 reliefs of 50 Inf. filling COWLANE – 60 Inf. carrying – 30 Inf clearing drains of WINE & HAYSTACK AVENUES –	
	Remainder in workshops –	
	102nd Fd Coy attached for instruction –	
	Night.	
	2/Lt. Barton & No 2 Sect. revetting BREASTWORK AV. & putting in look out posts in front line – 400 Inf. filling BREASTWORK AVENUE – 1 Sect. of 102nd Coy revetting WELLINGTON AVENUE.	

(73989) W4141—463. 400,000. 9/14. H.&J.Ltd. Forms/C. 2118/10.

Instructions regarding War Diaries and Intelligence Summaries are contained in F. S. Regs., Part II. and the Staff Manual respectively. Title pages will be prepared in manuscript.

WAR DIARY
or
INTELLIGENCE SUMMARY.
(Erase heading not required.)

Army Form C. 2118.

Hour, Date, Place	Summary of Events and Information	Remarks and references to Appendices
10. 9. 1915	Lt. Hall + No1 continued on 2 M.G. Shelters + re-revetted firing steps in S65-66 – 1 Sect. of 102nd Coy remodelling trench in 2nd S. Line by FARM DU BIEZ + 30 Inf. – 30 Inf. cleaning drains of WINE and COWGATE AVENUES – Pioneers laying floorboards in BREASTWORK AV. Remainder in workshops –	
	Night. Lt. Fowle + No4 laid sods on G.O.C's dug out – 1 Sect. of 102nd Coy revetting WELLINGTON AV – 30 Inf. carrying – 400 Inf filling BREASTWORK AV.	
11. 9. 15	Lt. Hall + No1 completed 2 shelters for M. Gunners in trench 59 – Put firing steps in COWGATE AV – Pioneers laying floorboards in BREASTWORK AV – 2 reliefs of 30 Inf. filling parados of LOWLANE – 1 Sect. of 102nd Coy + 2 reliefs of 30 Inf. on trench by FARM DU BIEZ – 30 Inf. filling roofs of M.G. Shelters + dug 2 new holes for others – Remainder in workshops –	
	Night. 2/Lt. Barton supervised 400 Inf. on BREASTWORK Av. + a carrying party of 30 Inf.	
12. 9. 15	Lieuts Fowle + Hall took Coy to ERQUINGHAM for baths.	
	2/Lt. Barton brought up pontoons + trestles from Bridging Train –	

Army Form C. 2118.

Instructions regarding War Diaries and Intelligence Summaries are contained in F. S. Regs., Part II. and the Staff Manual respectively. Title pages will be prepared in manuscript.

WAR DIARY
or
INTELLIGENCE SUMMARY.
(*Erase heading not required.*)

Hour, Date, Place	Summary of Events and Information	Remarks and references to Appendices
13. 9. 15.	Coy preparing to move - Major Gracey took O.C. 128th Fd Coy round trenches previously to handing over - night. 2/Lt. Barton & 1 Sect. 128th Coy revetting WELLINGTON AV -	
14. 9. 15.	Coy marched from RUE MARLE at 7.0 pm.	
15. 9. 15. STRAZEELE	Coy reached STRAZEE at 1.0 am - & went into billets.	
16. 9. 15	Lieuts Hall-Fowle & Barton took Coy for a route march in morning.	
17. 9. 15	Coy practicing ponton & trestle bridging in morning. 2/Lieut Williams & No 3. Sect rejoined the Coy	
18. 9. 15	Coy marched from STRAZEELE to THIENNES and entrained -	
19. 9. 15	Reached GUIANCOURT at 2.0 am. & detrained - Marched to CERISY & bivouaced till 9.30 am. then marched to FROISSY and bivouaced -	
20. 9. 15.	Major Gracey, Capt Sparkman & Lieuts Hall & Fowle went round part of new trenches by FRISE in morning -	
21. 9. 15.	Major Gracey, ~~Capt Sparkman~~ & Lieuts Hall & Fowle went round more trenches in morning - Capt Sparkman took transport & 2/Lt. Barton took the Coy to CAPPY. In aft. Major Gracey & Capt Sparkman reconnoitred part of the front line. Lt Hall reconnoitred a well & took 2/Lieuts	

(73989) W4141—463. 400,000. 9/14. H.&J.Ltd. Forms/C. 2118/10.

Instructions regarding War Diaries and Intelligence Summaries are contained in F. S. Regs., Part II. and the Staff Manual respectively. Title pages will be prepared in manuscript.

WAR DIARY
or
INTELLIGENCE SUMMARY.
(*Erase heading not required.*)

Army Form C. 2118.

Hour, Date, Place	Summary of Events and Information	Remarks and references to Appendices
	Williams & Barton round part of the trenches –	
22.9.15.	Capt. Spackman & Lieuts Hall & Fowle reconnoitred for positions for advanced Sections – Major Gracey & Capt. Spackman reconnoitred FRISE –	
	Aft. Major Gracey & O.C. K.R.R. visited a S. trench – Lt. Fowle & No 4 collected timber – Lt. Hall & No 1 commenced on dugouts for adv. Section.	
	~~Remainder, Drill~~ –	
	2/Lieut. Williams & ½ No 3 Sect. brought up materials from R.E. park at MERICOURT.	
	Remainder, Drill –	
	Night.	
	2/Lt. Barton supervised 200 Inf. digging S. Line at FRISE.	
	2/Lt. Williams & No 2 Sect. towed timber up canal –	
23.9.15.	Lt. Hall & No 1 commenced dugouts for adv. section in Rt. Sector & Lt. Fowle & No 4 – ditto in Lt. Sector.	
	2/Lt. Barton reconnoitred for cellars in CAPPY in event of bombardment.	
	Aft. No 2 Sect. went to bathe –	
	Major Gracey & Capt. Spackman reconnoitred front line.	
	Night.	
	2/Lt. Barton supervised 200 Inf. digging S. Line at FRISE.	
24.9.15.	Lt. Fowle & No 4 & ½ No 2 Sects. continued on dugouts. Lt. Hall & No 1 & ½ No 3 – ditto in rt. sector.	
	Night. 2/Lt. Barton supervised 50 Inf. on S. Line at FRISE.	

Instructions regarding War Diaries and Intelligence Summaries are contained in F. S. Regs., Part II. and the Staff Manual respectively. Title pages will be prepared in manuscript.

WAR DIARY
or
INTELLIGENCE SUMMARY.
(Erase heading not required.)

Army Form C. 2118.

Hour, Date, Place	Summary of Events and Information	Remarks and references to Appendices
25. 9. 1915.	Lieut Hall & Fowle same as yesterday – Capt. Spackman & Lt Hall reconnoitred centre of line –	
26. 9. 15.	R.C. Church parade in morning – night. 11 Lt. Barton supervised 200 inf. on S Line at FRISE & 40 inf. digging fire trench above ESPLANADE. 11 Lt. Williams & 1/2 No 3 put up breastwork revetment in marshes near FRISE & 1/2 No 3 hauling up timber.	
27. 9. 15	Lt. Fowle & No 4. continued on dugouts in Lt. sector. Capt. Spackman reconnoitred left sector & took over command of Lt Half Coy. Lt. Hall & Nos 1 & 2 continued on dugouts in rt. sector – night. 11 Lieuts Williams & Barton supervised 100 inf. deepening S. trench at FRISE & 70 inf. converting BOYAU DE FRANCE into a fire trench & continued a 'cut off' left of FRISE.	
28. 9. 15.	Lt. Fowle & No 4 went into adv. dugouts at FRISE – & 1/2 No 4 on dugouts & 1/2 on bridge over canal at FRISE – night. 11 Lt. Williams & No 3 wiring new trench in rear of FRISE & put up revetment for breastwork in rear of FRISE – 100 inf on S. trench left of BOYAU FRANCAIS – 70 on fire steps in BOYAU FRANCAIS – 100 inf. deepening ditto – 50 inf. carrying –	
29. 9. 15.	Lt Hall & No 1 went into & completed adv. dugouts in rt. sector. Lt. Fowle & 1/2 No 4 on bridge at FRISE & 1/2 No 4 revetting firing steps in S. trench left of BOYAU FRANCAIS.	

Instructions regarding War Diaries and Intelligence Summaries are contained in F. S. Regs., Part II. and the Staff Manual respectively. Title pages will be prepared in manuscript.

WAR DIARY
or
INTELLIGENCE SUMMARY.
(Erase heading not required.)

Army Form C. 2118.

Hour, Date, Place	Summary of Events and Information	Remarks and references to Appendices
29. 9. 15	night. 2/Lt. Barton supervised 100 inf. in ~~Commun~~ BOYAU DU SIGNAL. 2/Lt. Williams & ½ No3 improving fire trench behind craters & ½ wiring trench to rear of FRISE.	
30. 9. 15.	Lt. Hall & No1 commenced revetting S. Line of J.1 - Drained communication trench to MANSELL'S WOOD - Carried up materials. Lt. Fowle & ½ No4 on bridge at FRISE & ½ completed S. trench. night. 2/Lt. Barton & Lt. Hall supervised 150 inf. on BOYAU DU SIGNAL - 30 inf. on S. Line - 50 inf. on S. Line dugouts - 30 inf. carrying. No 2. Sect. wired S. line of J.1. 2/Lt. Williams & No3 improving S. Line behind Craters - supervised 130 inf. on BOYAU FRANCAIS - 80 on dugouts in S. line - 30 inf. filling breastwork at FRISE - 30 inf. carrying.	

27th Division

121/7381

M

17th Field Coy: RE

~~Vol XV~~

Oct 15

Instructions regarding War Diaries and Intelligence Summaries are contained in F. S. Regs., Part II. and the Staff Manual respectively. Title pages will be prepared in manuscript.

WAR DIARY
or
INTELLIGENCE SUMMARY.
(*Erase heading not required.*)

Army Form C. 2118.

Hour, Date, Place	Summary of Events and Information	Remarks and references to Appendices
	Confidential War Diary of 17th Field Coy RE for period Oct. 1st 1915 to Oct. 31st 1915.	HEADQUARTERS 2 NOV. 1915 482 27th DIVISIONAL ENGINEERS
	P. G. Spackman Capt RE for OC 17 Coy RE.	E. W. Noble Capt. RE Adjutant 27th Div Engrs for CRE 27th Div 2/11/15

(73989) W4141—463. 400,000. 9/14. H.&J.Ltd. Forms/C. 2118/10.

Instructions regarding War Diaries and Intelligence Summaries are contained in F. S. Regs., Part II. and the Staff Manual respectively. Title pages will be prepared in manuscript.

WAR DIARY
or
INTELLIGENCE SUMMARY.
(Erase heading not required.)

Army Form C. 2118.

1.

Hour, Date, Place	Summary of Events and Information	Remarks and references to Appendices
CAPPY. OCT. 1915 1st	Lieut Hall + ½ No1. Sect. revetting J.1.S. other half carrying up materials. 2/Lieut Barton + No2. cutting pickets at FROISSY. Lieut Irwle + No4 completed bridge at FRISE + revetted S. line steps. Pioneers cut timber at FROISSY.	
2nd	Lieut Hall + ½ No1. Sect. revetting J.1.S. + ½ carrying materials. No1 Sect. returned to CAPPY in evening. 2/Lieut Barton + No2 + 20 pioneers cut pickets + made hurdles at FROISSY. Lieut Irwle + No4 on S. line behind craters + returned to billets in evening. Night. 2/Lieut Barton supervised 70 Inf. making holes for dug-outs. 30 Inf. on S. line + 50 Inf. on Boyau du SIGNAL. 2/Lieut Williams supervised 80 Inf. on S. line dugout holes, 30 Inf. at FRISE, 100 on Boyau FRANCAIS, 30 Inf. on S. line.	
3rd	No2 + 3 Sects + Lieuts Barton + Williams went up to advanced dugouts in aft. Night. Lieut Hall supervised 100 Inf. on S. Line - 80 Inf. on holes for dugouts. Major Gracy + Lieut Hall reconnoitred S. Line wire. Lieut Irwle supervised 80 Inf. on holes for dugouts - 50 Inf. on S. Line and 30 at FRISE.	No 5876 2/Cpl A MacGregor wounded.

Instructions regarding War Diaries and Intelligence Summaries are contained in F. S. Regs., Part II. and the Staff Manual respectively. Title pages will be prepared in manuscript.

WAR DIARY
or
INTELLIGENCE SUMMARY.
(Erase heading not required.)

Army Form C. 2118.

2.

Hour, Date, Place	Summary of Events and Information	Remarks and references to Appendices
4th	2/Lieut Williams & No3 improving Gabion line & ½ No4 on S. line behind Craters. 40 Inf. on dugouts. 20 Inf. on cut off at FRISE & 20 Inf. filling sandbags.	
	Lieut Hall & No1 & pioneers cut pickets & made hurdles at FROISSY. 2/Lieut Barton & No2 revetting S. line - 50 Inf. carrying. 50 Inf. widening S. line & making firing steps.	
	Night. Lieut Irwin & ½ No4 improving Gabion line. 40 Inf. on new S. line. 50 Inf. holes for dugouts.	
	2/Lieut Barton supervised 100 Inf. joining gap in S. line. 50 Inf. holes for dugouts. 50 Inf. on Boyau de SIGNAL	
5th	2/Lieut Williams & No3 on Gabion line & ½ No4 on line behind	
	2/Lieut Barton & No2 revetting S. Line - 60 Inf. widening S. line & firing steps - 20 Inf. carrying.	
	Hall & [illegible] No1 & pioneers cut timber at FROISSY for dugouts. Remainder of No1 improved Bde Batt Hqrs.	
	Bn relief - no night work -	
6th	Lieut Hall & No1 sharpening pickets, cutting timber & making [illegible] Pioneers cutting pickets.	
	3 Inf. officers attached for instruction.	
	2/Lieut Barton & No2 commenced on S. line dugouts	

(73989) W4141—463. 400,000. 9/14. H.&J.Ltd. Forms/C. 2118/10.

Instructions regarding War Diaries and Intelligence Summaries are contained in F. S. Regs., Part II. and the Staff Manual respectively. Title pages will be prepared in manuscript.

WAR DIARY
or
INTELLIGENCE SUMMARY.
(Erase heading not required.)

Army Form C. 2118.

3.

Hour, Date, Place	Summary of Events and Information	Remarks and references to Appendices
6th	No 3 & 4 Sects continued on Gabion line & the lines behind K2. Nights. Lieut Hall & No 1 & Bde pioneers wiring Support line. 2/Lieut Baxter called up to investigate mining scare in J.3. 2/Lieut Williams supervised 60 Inf. on dugouts behind K.3 & 30 Inf. carrying timber for them	
7th	Lieut Hall instructed No 1 Sect & the pioneers in wiring in aft. No 1 also made hurdles & cut short pickets repaired "Bath house" Engine. Lieut Baxter & No 2 continued on S. Line dugouts & improving S. Line & 20 Inf. carrying. 2 reliefs of 40 Inf. on S. Line. 2/Lieut Williams & No 3 & 4 on Gabion line & lines behind K2. Nights. Lieut Fowle & 100 Inf. [illegible] for dugouts in K.2.S. 2/Lieut Baxter & 150 Inf. joining up gaps in S. Line.	
9th ~~8th~~ Apl.	Lieut Baxter & No 2 dugouts & improving S. Line. 2 reliefs of 20 Inf carrying. 2 reliefs of 30 Inf. improving S. Line. Capt. Spackman & Lieut Hall reconnoitred MANSELLS WOOD in aft. No 1 Sect. cutting timber. No 2 Sect returned to billets in evening.	

(73989) W4141—463. 400,000. 9/14. H.&J.Ltd. Forms/C. 2118/10.

Instructions regarding War Diaries and Intelligence Summaries are contained in F. S. Regs., Part II. and the Staff Manual respectively. Title pages will be prepared in manuscript.

WAR DIARY
or
INTELLIGENCE SUMMARY.
(Erase heading not required.)

Army Form C. 2118.

4

Hour, Date, Place	Summary of Events and Information	Remarks and references to Appendices
~~6th~~ 9th	2/Lieut Williams & Nos 3 & 4 on Galerie line & lines behind K2. Pioneers on BELLEVUE Trench. Bn reliefs. No night work.	
8th	2/Lieut Barton & No 2 continued on S. Line dugouts – 20 Inf. carrying 2 reliefs of 40 Inf. on S. Line. No 1 Sect cutting timber. Lieut. Fowle & Nos 3 & 4 continued on Galerie line & line behind craters.	
	Night. Lieut Hall 50 Inf on S. Line – Pioneers wiring T. 1. S. 2/Lieut Williams – 100 Inf on dugout holes behind K2 in S. Line.	
10th	Company had baths in morning. Nos 1 & 4 went up to advanced dugouts in evening.	
	Night. 2/Lieut Williams supervised 100 Inf on dugout holes behind K2 S. 2/Lieut Barton " 150 Inf on S Line of T2/T3.	
11th	Lieut Fowle & Nos 3 & 4 improving Bellevue – Ebonite & Galerie trenches & S Line with 140 Inf. Lieut Hall & No 1. Traverses & dugouts in T. 1 S. 2 reliefs of 20 Inf. carrying – 2 reliefs of 25 Inf. on dugouts – 2 reliefs of 30 Inf. fire steps in S. Line. Pioneers fire steps in T 1 S. 12 Inf. well sinking – 2/Lieut Barton & No 2 cut timber at FROISSY.	

Instructions regarding War Diaries and Intelligence Summaries are contained in F. S. Regs., Part II. and the Staff Manual respectively. Title pages will be prepared in manuscript.

WAR DIARY
or
INTELLIGENCE SUMMARY.
(Erase heading not required.)

Army Form C. 2118.

5.

Hour, Date, Place	Summary of Events and Information	Remarks and references to Appendices
11th	Night.	
	2/Lieut Williams supervised 100 Inf. in dugouts behind S. Line & Gabion line.	
	Lieut Hall. 20 Inf. holes for dugouts & 10 Inf. in T. 3. S.	
12th	No 3 sections & 200 Inf. same as 11th. Lieut. Hall & No 1 traverses revetting firesteps & parapet of T. 1. S. – 12 Inf. well sinking – 2 reliefs of 50 Inf. carrying – 2 reliefs of 35 Inf. in S. Line	
	2/Lieut Barton & No 2 cut timber – Cpl Pelham instructed pioneers in wiring	
	Night.	
	2/Lt Barton & No 2 wiring S. Line – 30 Inf. carrying.	
13th	Lieut Hall & No 1 – traverses revetting firesteps & parapet of T. 1. S. – 20 Inf. squaring up dugout holes – 50 Inf. filling Sandbags & assisting on S. Line – 12 Inf. well sinking.	
	2/Lt Barton & No 2 & pioneers cleared up wood at FROISSY.	
	No 3 sect & 200 Inf. same as 11th.	
	No night work owing to Bn relief.	
14th	No 3 & 4 + 250 Inf. as on 11th Lt Hall & No 1 same as 13th. No work on well owing to foul air – Pioneers carrying – 2/Lt Barton & No 2 revetted dugouts in T. 1. S.	

(73989) W4141—463. 400,000. 9/14. H.&J.Ltd. Forms/C. 2118/10.

Instructions regarding War Diaries and Intelligence Summaries are contained in F. S. Regs., Part II. and the Staff Manual respectively. Title pages will be prepared in manuscript.

WAR DIARY
or
INTELLIGENCE SUMMARY.
(Erase heading not required.)

Army Form C. 2118.

6.

Hour, Date, Place	Summary of Events and Information	Remarks and references to Appendices
14th	Night. 2/Lt. Williams supervised 40 inf. carrying. Lieut. Hall supervised 20 inf. in T. 3. S. – 25 inf. holes for dugouts – 40 inf. levelling off parapet – ½ No 1 Sect. revetting parapet of T. 1. S.	
15th	2/Lieut. Williams went on leave. Lieut. Fowle + Nos 3 + 4 + 2 reliefs of 200 inf. as on 11th. River rising at FRISE + being unable to open lock gates on sluices Capt. Sparkman blew a hole in lock gate. Lieut. Hall + No 1 + pioneers as on 14th. 2 reliefs of 100 inf. assisting in S. Line – 12 inf. fixed blower + continued on well. 2/Lt. Barton + No 2 cleared up wood at FROISSY. Night. Lt. Hall supervised 25 inf. on holes for dugouts + 28 inf. levelling parapet of T. 1. S.	
16th	2/Lt. Barton + No 2 cleared up wood at FROISSY. Lieut. Hall + No 1 traverses revetted firesteps in S. Line + completed 3 dugouts + revetted parapet. 30 inf. firesteps in T. 2. S. 50 inf. carrying. 12 inf. worked on well. Nos 1 + 4 returned to billets in evening. Nos 3 + 4 + 50 inf. as on 11th	

(73989) W4141—463. 400,000. 9/14. H.&J.Ltd. Forms/C. 2118/10.

Instructions regarding War Diaries and Intelligence Summaries are contained in F. S. Regs., Part II. and the Staff Manual respectively. Title pages will be prepared in manuscript.

WAR DIARY
or
INTELLIGENCE SUMMARY.
(Erase heading not required.)

Army Form C. 2118.

2

Hour, Date, Place	Summary of Events and Information	Remarks and references to Appendices
17th	Company had baths in morning. Lieut Fowle & 2/Lt Barton went up to advanced dugouts with No 3 + 2 in evening.	
18th	2/Lt Barton & No 2 revetted parapet of T 2 S. Lt Hall & No 1 collected timber from FROISSY. Lt Fowle & No 3 + 4 with 2 reliefs of 100 Inf. as before. night. 2/Lt Barton supervised 50 Inf. on holes for dugouts – 150 Inf on new Cm Trench from Boyau du Signal to Maxwell's Wood.	Work in the left Sector was carried on under very difficult & trying circumstances owing to the enemy's liberality of bombs & grenades –
19th	Lieut Fowle & No 3 + 4 & 100 Inf started on Trenches Ebovles, Bellevue, & trench in front of Fortin but owing to heavy bombing had to knock off. No 4 then worked on dugouts & No 3 continued on Fortin & Eboulis at night. Lieut Hall instructed pioneers in wiring & sandbagging. 2/Lt Barton & No 2 revetting S. Line. 30 Inf. widening & deepening Boyau du Signal & 50 deepening T 2 S – 50 filling sandbags & 50 carrying night. Lt Hall & No 1 wiring S. Line.	
20th	2/Lt Barton & No 2 & pioneers deepening T 2 S. re-revetting firesteps & sandbagging parapet. Lieut Fowle & No 3 on K3 S. & No 4 in K2 dugouts. Pioneers on Bellevue – No Inf. or night work owing to relief –	

Instructions regarding War Diaries and Intelligence Summaries are contained in F. S. Regs., Part II. and the Staff Manual respectively. Title pages will be prepared in manuscript.

WAR DIARY
or
INTELLIGENCE SUMMARY.
(Erase heading not required.)

Army Form C. 2118.

8.

Hour, Date, Place	Summary of Events and Information	Remarks and references to Appendices
21st	Lieut Hall & No 1 cut timber at FROISSY then went on to MERICOURT & brought back pontoons & trestles to CAPPY. 2/Lt. Barton & No 2 traverses revetting T. 2. S. 200 Inf in aft. improving T2/T3 S. Boyau the Signal & 8 line dugouts. Work on well stopped by G.O.C. orders.	
22nd	Lieut Fowle & 2/Lt Barton with Inf. Working Parties moved stores from R.E. dumps & left them i/c of Bns	
23rd	Company pontooning & trestling all day. 2/Lieut Wells came returned from leave.	
24th	C. of E. parade.	
25th	Company pontooning in morning. 2/Lt Barton & some of No 2 went on to take over & clean up tomorrows billets.	
26th	Coy marched from CAPPY to billets on PERONNE Rd about 1½ M. S. of MORCOURT. Major Gracey went on leave	
27th	Coy marched to camp at BOVES.	
28th	Coy struck camp & marched to FLUY.	

(73989) W4141—463. 400,000. 9/14. H.&J.Ltd. Forms/C. 2118/10.

Army Form C. 2118.

Instructions regarding War Diaries and Intelligence Summaries are contained in F. S. Regs., Part II. and the Staff Manual respectively. Title pages will be prepared in manuscript.

WAR DIARY
or
INTELLIGENCE SUMMARY.

(Erase heading not required.)

9.

Hour, Date, Place	Summary of Events and Information	Remarks and references to Appendices
29th	Company pontooning & trestling in morning.	
30th	Company did a route march in morning, and pontooning & trestling in afternoon.	
31st	C. of E. parade in morning	

(73989) W4141—463. 400,000. 9/14. H.&J.Ltd. Forms/C. 2118/10.

27th Div

17th F. Co. R.E.

Nov

Vol XVI

121/7663

Army Form C. 2118.

Instructions regarding War Diaries and Intelligence Summaries are contained in F. S. Regs., Part II. and the Staff Manual respectively. Title pages will be prepared in manuscript.

WAR DIARY
or
INTELLIGENCE SUMMARY

(Erase heading not required.)

Hour, Date, Place	Summary of Events and Information	Remarks and references to Appendices
	Confidential War Diary of 17th Field Coy RE. for period Nov 1st to 30th. 1915. [illegible] Maj RE Comdg 17th Field Coy RE 5/12/15	[illegible] Lieut. Col. R.E. C.R.E. 27th Division

1247 W 3299 200,000 (E) 8/14 J.B.C. & A. Forms/C. 2118/11.

Army Form C. 2118.

Instructions regarding War Diaries and Intelligence Summaries are contained in F. S. Regs., Part II. and the Staff Manual respectively. Title pages will be prepared in manuscript.

WAR DIARY
or
INTELLIGENCE SUMMARY.
(Erase heading not required.)

1.

Hour, Date, Place	Summary of Events and Information	Remarks and references to Appendices
FLUY – NOVEMBER 1915 1st	Borrowed pontoons from 2nd WESSEX 7th Coy to put whole day pontooning & instruction in knotting and lashing.	
2nd	Route March in morning.	
3rd	Major Gray returned from & Capt. Sparkman went on leave. Lieuts Hall & Fowle checked Coy tools, stores & equipment. 2nd Lieuts Williams & Barton took Coy for a route march.	
4th	Pontooning & instruction in derricks, shears etc in morning. Drill in afternoon.	
5th	Right Half Coy erecting derricks etc. Left half Coy route march in morning. Coy cleaned up picket lines in aft. Lieut Fowle went on leave.	
6th	Left half Coy erecting derricks etc. Right Half Coy route march in morning.	
7th	Church of England parade at REVELLES in morning.	

Instructions regarding War Diaries and Intelligence Summaries are contained in F. S. Regs., Part II. and the Staff Manual respectively. Title pages will be prepared in manuscript.

WAR DIARY
or
INTELLIGENCE SUMMARY.
(Erase heading not required.)

Army Form C. 2118.

2

Hour, Date, Place	Summary of Events and Information	Remarks and references to Appendices
8th	Kit equipment inspection & drill in morning. 2nd Lieut Ross arrived –	
9th	Section, musketry & company drill in morning. Capt. Spackman returned from leave.	
10th	Route march in morning. Lieut Fowle returned from & 2nd Lieut. ~~William~~ Barton went on leave. 2nd Lieut Williams transferred to 20th Fortress Coy	
11th	Route march in morning.	
12th	Route march in morning. Lieut Hall started for leave.	
13th	Route march in morning. Capt. Spackman drew mules for Coy. Lieut Hall returned as leave boat stopped.	
14th	C of E. parade cancelled owing to rain.	
15th	Route March in morning	
16th	Rehearsal marching order parade in morning 2nd Lieut Barton returned from leave 2nd Lieut Coombs arrived –	

Instructions regarding War Diaries and Intelligence Summaries are contained in F. S. Regs., Part II. and the Staff Manual respectively. Title pages will be prepared in manuscript.

WAR DIARY
or
INTELLIGENCE SUMMARY.
(Erase heading not required.)

3.

Army Form C. 2118.

Hour, Date, Place	Summary of Events and Information	Remarks and references to Appendices
17th	Route March in morning. 2/Lieut Ross transferred to 7th Fd Coy RE.	
18th	Route march in morning.	
19th	Route march in morning. Lieut Hall went on leave.	
20th	Route March in morning	
21st	C. of E. parade in morning Lieut Fowle went on leave.	
22nd & 23rd	Route March in morning.	
24th	Drill in morning.	
25th	Route march in morning. Hall returned from leave.	
26th	Drill in morning. Washed wagons in afternoon Lieut Fowle returned from leave.	
27th	Route march in morning	
28th	Nil – No padre available for church	
29th & 30th	Route march in ~~afternoon~~ morning	

(73989) W4141—463. 400,000. 9/14. H.&J.Ltd. Forms/C. 2118/10.

27

17th Fd. Co. R.E.

Dec

Vol. XVII

27b

Instructions regarding War Diaries and Intelligence Summaries are contained in F. S. Regs., Part II. and the Staff Manual respectively. Title pages will be prepared in manuscript.

WAR DIARY
or
INTELLIGENCE SUMMARY.
(*Erase heading not required.*)

Army Form C. 2118.

1

Hour, Date, Place	Summary of Events and Information	Remarks and references to Appendices
FLUY. Dec. 1st 2nd 3rd & 4th	Route March in morning.	
5th	No Church parade as no padre available.	
6th	Marching order parade.	
7th	Marched from FLUY to LONGEAU STATION and entrained. Left at 7.15 p.m.	
8th	En route.	
MARSEILLES. 9th	Detrained at MARSEILLES at 6.30 pm & marched to camp.	
10th	Camp fatigues.	
11th	Company had baths in morning. Night Lieuts Hall & [illegible] & 25 men from both No 1 & No 4 section patrolled MARSEILLES under A.P.M.	
12th	C. of E. parade.	
13th	Nos 1 & 3 Sections on A.S.C. fatigues. No 2 & 4 route march. Moved from EXHIBITION CAMP to CAMP BORELY in aft.	
14th	Route march	
15th	Camp fatigues.	
16th	Route march	
17th & 18th	Camp fatigues.	

Instructions regarding War Diaries and Intelligence Summaries are contained in F. S. Regs., Part II. and the Staff Manual respectively. Title pages will be prepared in manuscript.

WAR DIARY
or
INTELLIGENCE SUMMARY.

(*Erase heading not required.*)

Army Form C. 2118.

2

Hour, Date, Place		Summary of Events and Information	Remarks and references to Appendices
MARSEILLES	19th	C of E parade. Afternoon Lieut Fowle & ½ No 1 Sect. went as firing party to a soldier's funeral.	
	20th 21st	Route march & fatigues	
	22nd	Route march. Night 2nd Lieut Coombs & ½ No 3 Section police picquet under A.P.M.	
	23rd	Route march	
	24th	Route march & fatigues. Coy provided DOCK guard.	
	25th	C of E parade	
	26th	Nil —	
	27th	Route march & fatigues	
	28th	Fatigues	
	29th & 30th	Route march & fatigues	
	31st	Route march & fatigues. Capt Spackman took pontoons & trestles of all 3 Fd Coys to DOCKS for embarkation.	
		[illegible] Maj RE O.C. 17th Coy RE 1.1.16	

(73989) W4141—463. 400,000. 9/14. H.&J.Ltd. Forms/C. 2118/10.

www.ingramcontent.com/pod-product-compliance
Lightning Source LLC
Chambersburg PA
CBHW081439160426
43193CB00013B/2329
9781474513876